ESCAPING OCCUPIED EUROPE

A DUTCHMAN'S DANGEROUS JOURNEY TO JOIN THE ALLIES

GW00392009

ESCAPING OCCUPIED EUROPE

A DUTCHMAN'S DANGEROUS JOURNEY TO JOIN THE ALLIES

AS WRITTEN BY DANIËL DE MOULIN

HYLKE FABER AND PIETER STOLK

TRANSLATED BY DIEKE VAN WIJNEN
REPUBLIC OF LETTERS TRANSLATIONS

PEN & SWORD
HISTORY

AN IMPRINT OF PEN & SWORD BOOKS LTD
YORKSHIRE – PHILADELPHIA

Originally published in Dutch by Stichting DdM, 2006
as
Wij zijn niet bang, tenminste, niet erg.
Het Engelandvaardersdagboek van
Daniël de Moulin
Second revised edition DdM Works, 2015

First published in Great Britain in 2018 by
PEN AND SWORD HISTORY
an imprint of
Pen & Sword Books Ltd
Yorkshire - Philadelphia

ISBN 978 1 52674 122 6

Typeset in Sabon 11/13.5 By
Aura Technology and Software Services, India
Printed and bound by TJ International Ltd.

Pen & Sword Books Ltd incorporates the Imprints of Pen & Sword Books
Archaeology, Atlas, Aviation, Battleground, Discovery, Family History, History,
Maritime, Military, Naval, Politics, Railways, Select, Transport, True Crime,
Fiction, Frontline Books, Leo Cooper, Praetorian Press, Seaforth Publishing,
Wharncliffe and White Owl.

For a complete list of Pen & Sword titles please contact

PEN & SWORD BOOKS LIMITED
47 Church Street, Barnsley, South Yorkshire, S70 2AS, England
E-mail: enquiries@pen-and-sword.co.uk
Website: www.pen-and-sword.co.uk
or
PEN AND SWORD BOOKS
1950 Lawrence Rd, Havertown, PA 19083, USA
E-mail: Uspen-and-sword@casematepublishers.com

Contents

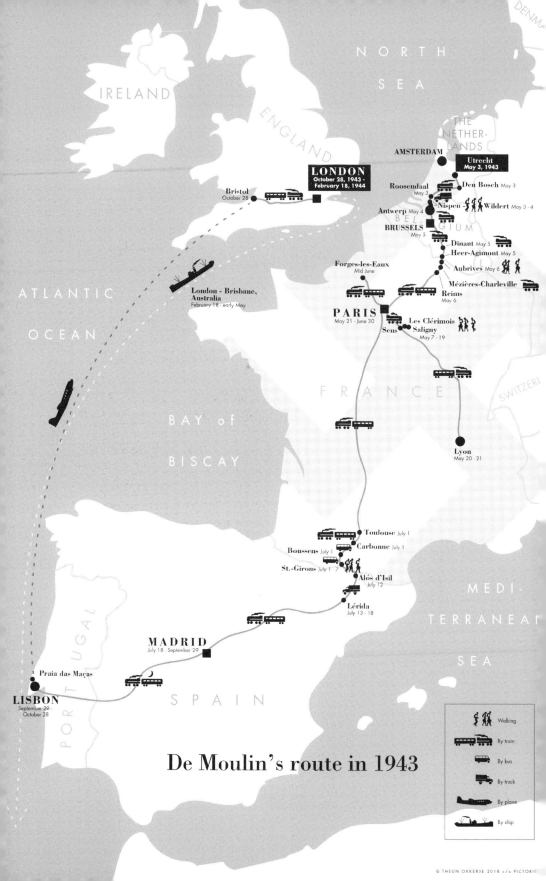

De Moulin's route in 1943

N O R T H

S E A

IRELAND

ENGLAND

DENMARK

THE
NETHER-
LANDS

AMSTERDAM

Utrecht
May 3, 1943

LONDON
October 28, 1943 -
February 18, 1944

Bristol
October 28

Roosendaal
May 3

Den Bosch May 3

Nispen

Wildert May 3 - 4

Antwerp May 4

BELGIUM

BRUSSELS
May 5

Dinant May 5

Heer-Agimont May 5

Aubrives May 6

Mézières-Charleville

Forges-les-Eaux
Mid June

Reims
May 6

London - Brisbane,
Australia
February 18 - early May

ATLANTIC

OCEAN

PARIS
May 21 - June 30

Les Clérimois
Saligny
May 7 - 19

Sens

BAY of

BISCAY

F R A N C E

SWITZERL

Lyon
May 20 - 21

Toulouse July 1

Carbonne July 1

Boussens July 1

St.-Girons July 1 - 7

Alós d'Isil
July 12

MEDI-

TERRANEA

SEA

Lérida
July 13 - 18

MADRID
July 18 -
September 29

Praia das Maças

SPAIN

LISBON
September 29 -
October 28

PORTUGAL

Walking

By train

By bus

By truck

By plane

By ship

© THEUN OKKERSE 2018 c/o PICTORIC

Editors' Note

On 9 July 2008, exactly sixty-five years after Daniël De Moulin crossed the French-Spanish border in the Pyrenees, we crossed the same mountains in his footsteps with this travelogue as our guide. It was the culmination of almost five years of work during weekends, holidays and evenings, in which we pieced together De Moulin's story. Now, ten years later, we are proud to share De Moulin's words and the history of those men and women who escaped to England during the Second World War, the so-called *Engelandvaarders*, with an international audience. The travelogue you have in your hands was written in London in February 1944 by Daniël de Moulin after his *Engelandvaart*.

Our quest which led to this book began at a fraternity in Utrecht, the very same place where, in a long-lost past, De Moulin himself had set foot. We knew that he had escaped to England and that he had played a role in the student resistance movement in Utrecht, but that was really all we knew. The sheer lack of information aroused our curiosity; we wanted to try and paint a picture of a period in the life of someone who resembled us both in terms of age and background, but who had been forced to make decisions that for us seemed unthinkable. Because some friends of De Moulin were still alive at that moment, this appeared to us to be a perfect opportunity to collect the still available pieces of the puzzle relating to De Moulin's war history.

Initially, we concluded our research in May of 2005 with a short article. Through interviews and archival research, we had succeeded in piecing together the historical facts, but felt we had not been successful in giving it colour. In particular, there were gaps in the reconstruction of the journey to London due to the lack of personal details. However, not long afterwards, De Moulin's personal travelogue was found in his widow's estate. Now we possessed the story we had been searching for. The first Dutch edition of the travelogue was published in May 2006. Nine years later, in 2015 we published the second revised edition.

Why bother telling this story almost seventy-five years after the end of the Second World War? Unlike many war stories, this is not a 'big story' full of fighting and death-defying heroic actions. As far as we know, De Moulin was not involved in the violent resistance in the occupied Netherlands. On the contrary, he was part of the 'intellectual resistance' by students and professors. De Moulin's journey to England was special, but certainly not unique.

At the same time, that in itself is exactly where the value of his text lies. De Moulin's travelogue is the story of a 20-year-old who found himself in a situation which, for him, was no longer tenable and forced him to leave the Netherlands and join the Allied forces. The lively way in which De Moulin describes his preparations and his poignant and humorous descriptions of those who shared his fate make the text exceptionally interesting and worth reading for today's audience.

In addition to the full text of the travelogue, this book also includes supporting chapters and appendices, which provide the context for De Moulin's story. The first chapter sketches the background of his life as a student in Utrecht and his activities during the first part of the war. The next chapter draws a picture of the *Engelandvaarders*, their reasons for leaving the Netherlands, and how they reached England. Finally, there is a summary of De Moulin's life after his journey to England, as well as that of his travel companions Lodewijk Parren and Rolande Kloesmeijer.

Whilst this publication gives a detailed picture of *Engelandvaarder* De Moulin, we know very little about the exact content of his resistance work which was, in part, what drove him to leave the Netherlands in May 1943. To a certain extent, this is not surprising; there are many people about whom not much is known regarding the details of their resistance work during the war. After the war, this was a subject that many were unwilling to discuss. Hence, information about it in written sources is limited and many of those who were indirectly involved in it and with whom we spoke, could not remember the details after so many years.

De Moulin begins his story by saying that the travelogue was only intended for his immediate family. Although we obviously did not respect his wishes by publishing this book, we believe that our goal in doing so, and the fact that so much time has passed since it was written, justifies our choice. Our decision was determined by our belief that this publication does not violate either his memory or that of his loved ones.

Editors' Note

In fact, in publishing this book we seek to keep alive the memory of Daniël de Moulin and the many who chose to put their lives at risk to regain our freedom. We hope that you will enjoy reading De Moulin's travelogue and that it will give you the opportunity to not only reflect on this story, but also on the many other stories which have never been told, or never will be.

Amsterdam, 9 July 2018

Hylke Faber
Pieter Stolk

Chapter 1

A Student in Wartime

'Sir, sir, open up! We are at war!' It was with these words that the Utrecht student Daniël de Moulin's landlady woke him on 10 May 1940. That morning, Operation *Fall Gelb* (Case Yellow) had begun: German troops pushed through the Netherlands, Belgium, Luxembourg and France in an overwhelming attack to subdue Western Europe. Now, the Second World War had begun for the Netherlands.

De Moulin and *Unitas*

Eight months earlier, in September 1939, Daniël de Moulin had begun his studies in medicine at Utrecht University in the Netherlands. At the start of his studies, he had become a member of the Utrecht student association called *Unitas Studiosorum Rheno-Traiectina* (USR). Within the USR, as in mixed student associations elsewhere in the Netherlands, it was customary for members to band together in so-called 'year clubs'. These clubs were small groups consisting of about eight people; they were usually of the same sex and had joined the USR in the same year. Together they organized a variety of activities, and were the source for many friendships. Daniël was a member of the year club *Inter nos*, a club of six men, of which four members would become active in the student resistance during the war. Three of them would eventually escape to England.

Particular to *Inter Nos* was the fact that, like De Moulin, most of its members had some connection to the Dutch East Indies. Daniël was born in Bogor, West-Java, on 12 September 1919 where his father was Professor of Anatomy at the Dutch East Indies veterinary school. Prior to beginning his studies in Utrecht, De Moulin had returned to the Netherlands with his parents, his younger brother Peter and his sister Eleonara; they settled in the town of Naarden.

The *Symposion* clubhouse of the USR student association at Lucas Bolwerk 8 in Utrecht, 1937.

First year students in 1939 at the Unitas S.R. student association clubhouse, *Symposion*, including Daniël de Moulin and his year club members Wim Heirsch and Armand Berg. Note the uniformed student due to the Dutch mobilization of August 1939.

Accommodation

Even though the *Wehrmacht* (the armed forces of Nazi Germany) encountered powerful opposition, as a result of which its offensive stalled at various places, the Dutch resistance was broken five days after the invasion on 10 May. After the bombing of Rotterdam on 14 May, which destroyed almost the entire historic city centre, and killed nearly 900 people and made 85,000 others homeless, it was clear that continuing to fight for a few days more would not weigh up against the sheer number of the resulting civilian casualties, particularly now that the Germans had threatened to bomb Utrecht, the second largest city of the Netherlands. The Netherlands surrendered on 15 May.

Before the war, De Moulin was declared unfit for service due to his eyesight and he could therefore not take part in combat operations himself, something he deeply regretted. He had spent the days after the German invasion looking for a place where he might be of assistance.

12

However, neither the voluntary militia nor the Red Cross could use his help. For the time being, all he could do was wait.

After surrendering, Dutch society took on a 'wait and see' attitude: they waited to see how the German authorities would behave and how the war would affect their personal lives. About this De Moulin wrote: 'Initially the Germans kept quiet and the Dutch hoped that the occupation would prove to be of a military nature only and that – with certain restrictions such as rationing and blackouts, of course – life would go on as normal.'

Amongst the students in those days, discussion centred around the stand one should take. For example, could German students be welcomed at the various student associations in the city? Was one allowed to give money to the Dutch Nazi organization, Winter Relief (a charitable organisation providing relief to the poor)? The traditional rivalry between the student associations, an important pastime before the war, was pushed to the background in light of the occupation.

Nonetheless, teaching at the university continued. After the war, De Moulin said of this: 'We went back to our studies; what else could we do?' Although the first weeks of the occupation passed quietly, soon afterwards the Germans announced their first measures. And, although these were based on religion, not race, their real purpose soon became clear. In November 1940, Jewish employees were dismissed from their jobs, temporarily retaining full pay. That decision led to a lot of resistance among the students and professors. In Leiden the measures led to non-Jewish professor, Cleveringa giving an influential speech in which he publicly protested the dismissal of Jewish employees. Consequently, in Delft and Leiden student strikes broke out. Therefore the German authorities closed these two universities. In the meantime, the Academic Board of Utrecht University strove at all costs to prevent a strike from taking place in order to avoid closure of the university. Rector Magnificus Kruyt, the chancellor of Utrecht University, had a pamphlet circulated with the words 'even if one feels hurt, one does not commit suicide'.

The response of the board of Utrecht University to the unrest in Delft and Leiden is characteristic of the situation there during the occupation. In these dark days, the policy set by the Academic Board appears to have had as its highest goal to be able to operate as an independent institute as long as possible. To calm things down further, the board decided that the Christmas holidays should begin earlier than usual, on 6 December 1940.

DE RECTOR MAGNIFICUS
AAN DE UTRECHTSCHE STUDENTEN

Ik doe een beroep op Uw zelfbeheersching.
Ik ken Uw aanhankelijkheid aan Uw leer-
meesters evengoed als Gij de mijne voor
mijn collega's weet; ik begrijp ook, dat de
wensch in U leeft Uw gevoelens te uiten.
Maar ik doe een DRINGEND BEROEP op
U dat niet te doen door middelen, die onze
Universiteit schaden.
De Universiteit is een stuk Nederlandsche
volkskracht en in deze zware tijden moeten
wij elke Nederlandsche waarde hoog houden. Ook al voelt men zich gewond, daarom
slaat men toch niet de hand aan zich zelf.

**Uw hoogleeraren, die zich van hun verant-
woordelijkheid even goed rekenschap geven
als Gij, gaan door college te geven. Toont
Gij U met hen solidair door de colleges en
de instituten te blijven bezoeken.**

KRUYT

Pamphlet by Rector Magnificus Kruyt of Utrecht University.

THE RECTOR MAGNIFICUS
TO ALL UTRECHT STUDENTS

I am appealing to your self-control.

I know of your great affection for your teachers as you know of mine for my colleagues. I understand your desire to express your feelings, but I urge you not to do so by means which may harm our University.

The University is a measure of our strength as Dutch people and in hard times like these we must uphold our Dutch values. We do not kill ourselves just because we feel wounded.

Your professors, who take just as full an account of their responsibilities as you do, continue to lecture. Demonstrate your solidarity with them and persist in going to the institutes and attending the lectures.

KRUYT

14

Nascent resistance

Initially, resistance in the Netherlands was not organized well and only took place on a small scale: taking off one's hat when the traffic light turned orange (thereby showing one's respect for the House of Orange, the Dutch Royal Family), by giving German soldiers the wrong directions when the opportunity arose, or by celebrating Prince Bernhard's birthday on 29 June ('Carnation Day') by wearing a carnation, the prince's trademark, in their buttonholes. These were just a few examples of how the Dutch openly demonstrated their dissatisfaction with the German occupation.

De Moulin, too, contributed his bit to the resistance. With his brother Peter, he decided to seize Queen Wilhelmina's birthday as the occasion to express his aversion to the German occupation. On Saturday, 30 August 1941, Daniël and Peter left their parent's home in

The chimney of the steam laundry following the nocturnal activities of the De Moulin brothers.

the dark armed with a long piece of rope, white paint and a baton. In Naarden, where their parents lived, stood a factory building belonging to the *Gooische Stoomwasserij* (the steam laundry in the Gooi region), which was recognizable from afar because of its tall chimney. While Daniël kept watch, Peter, the more athletic of the two men, climbed up the chimney and painted the words 'Oranje Boven' on the chimney, referring to the Dutch flag with orange streamer and the House of Orange-Nassau - the Dutch royal dynasty from which its kings & queens derived. That day, the text was visible from a long distance, to the great annoyance of both the Germans and the supporters of the National Socialist Movement in the Netherlands (NSB).

Clandestine student association life

Pressure from the occupiers on the academic community increased during 1941. Jewish employees were dismissed in February and in the very same month, a measure was announced dictating that the number

Notification: The Executive Board, Board for the Clubhouse and members [of student association Unitas S.R.] are strictly forbidden to enter the clubhouse. The Tenant.

16

of Jewish students at the university could not exceed 3 per cent. Despite the Academic Board's fear of protests, everything remained calm. Only a few professors and the student newspapers paid public attention to the measure. Soon afterwards, these student newspapers were banned. On 18 June 1941, the authorities also banned the student associations which were 'nurseries and hotbeds for those with anti-German sentiments.' The societies were forbidden and their buildings sealed off on 11 July and then allocated to German and National Socialist organizations. The clubhouse of the USR, of which Daniel was a member and which was located in the historic centre of Utrecht, became home to the National Youth Storm, the youth section of the NSB.

Following their official dissolution, the student associations began an underground life and became more intertwined with the resistance's activities. With this, De Moulin's participation in student resistance began. A clandestine student board proved to be essential to the various student associations because the names of the regular board

The *College of Ephors* on the evening of its foundation. From left to right: Armand Berg, Daniël de Moulin, Connie van der Capellen, Lodewijk Parren and Wim Heirsch.

members were known to the authorities. Leadership of the association was therefore generally assigned to a secret board. This was also true of the USR. The *College of Ephors* was founded here; it was named after the Spartan rulers in ancient Greece. The rector (chairman) of the USR, Connie van der Cappellen, asked De Moulin to lead this college. This may have had something to do with the fact that both men shared a common Dutch East Indies past: Van der Cappellen, too, had come from the colonies. Shortly after the war he would return there as a government official and be killed in an ambush.

Van der Cappellen installed De Moulin and three of his year club members on 15 May 1942. Their mission was 'to represent all USR affairs in wartime and to prepare for re-establishment after the war.' De Moulin chose people from his network of friends because by doing so they were less likely to be noticed, and also because the risk of a leak would be smaller.

Origin of the nationwide student protest

The student associations and the clandestine association boards slowly started to form the core of the national student resistance. At a local level, the resistance in university and college towns was organized around a Council of Representatives. At a national level, there was the umbrella Council of Nine headed by John Albert Andrée Wiltens, from Utrecht. De Moulin took a seat in the local council on behalf of the USR and thus became closely linked to the student resistance at a national level.

According to De Moulin, the aim of the Council of Nine and the Council of Representatives was 'not to carry out acts of sabotage or other forms of violence, but rather to promote a mentality that would make it possible to take a sure and disciplined stand against the anticipated measures against the university and its students'.

At first the Council of Representatives was primarily busy with setting up communication systems for the distribution of messages and illegally printed newsletters and papers. One of the most important documents that was distributed was the illegal student newsletter, *De Geus onder studenten* (The Freedom Fighter among the students). This paper became the mouthpiece of the student resistance. Eventually it became possible to mobilize the student population using the established system whenever events gave rise to this.

De Moulin and the student resistance

Within the USR, De Moulin was occupied not only with organizing association meetings, but also with setting up a messaging system for the association. This system was used both for the dissemination of general messages relating to the war, as well as for other, more practical goals. For example, the system proved to be an excellent way to collect membership fees and distribute the yearbook. This yearbook was printed illegally in Rotterdam in 1942 and the cover was made from blackout paper, originally used to minimize outdoor light to prevent enemy aircraft from being able to identify their targets.

An activity which De Moulin and Parren proudly mention in a later testimony about the student resistance is, remarkably, the prevention of a protest action *against* a National Socialist organization. On 14 November, the National Socialist Student Front wanted to induct a group of new members in the auditorium of the University Hall. A pamphlet calling for violent protest against this was intercepted and destroyed by the student resistance; it would only have had the reverse effect and have led to severe reprisals by the Germans.

De Moulin's house at Brigittenstraat 20a, in Utrecht, was a centre of student resistant activity at that time. It was, for example, an assembly point for the various courier services. Later during the war, after De Moulin had left for England, an illegal telephone exchange was housed in the building

Lighter activities also took place here, such as the induction of USR's new recruits and rehearsals for stage performances. Part of the association's property could also be found here, such as valuable furniture and various items of a more symbolic value. After the clubhouse was sealed off by the Germans, nocturnal break-ins by students secured these items. In addition to the activities held at the Brigittenstraat, parties were also regularly organized elsewhere in the city. Due to the curfew, these parties had to last until the next morning, something which was probably not always experienced as 'punishment'. Among the party guests in the photos from the time one regularly sees police officers; they were given an alcoholic beverage as thanks for their efforts in leaving the events unrecorded in their reports.

Clandestine partying in Daan's room at Brigittenstraat 20a. Note the police officer in uniform (fourth from right).

Daniël playing the piano in his room at Brigittenstraat 20a.

Inter nos year club party in Lodewijks room at Lange Nieuwstraat 103. The chairs were the ceremonial chairs of the USR's board, secured by, among others, Lodewijk.

Lodewijk - the year club's photographer - taking pictures at Brigittenstraat 20a.

Rijksuniversiteit
   Utrecht
Domplein 29

Utrecht, **24 DEC. 1942**

Na den brand, welke in het Inschrijvingsbureau van de Rijksuniversiteit plaats vond, zal het inschrijvingsregister gereconstrueerd worden.

Daartoe zijn een aantal gegevens aanwezig. Enkele andere ontbreken.

Teneinde over deze laatste de beschikking te herkrijgen, wordt U bijgaand formulier toegezonden, **MET OPDRACHT** dit formulier, dubbel ingevuld, **binnen 3 dagen na dagteekening** dezes terug te zenden.

Daartoe wordt een portvrij couvert bijgevoegd.

De Rector-Magnificus
L. van Vuuren.

K 2372

Pamphlet requesting all students to send their personal information.

The Bureau of Registrations of Utrecht University is to be rebuilt following the fire which took place there.

Some of the information held by the Bureau has survived and can be used, but other information is missing.

It is with a view to recovering that which was lost that you are now being sent the attached form requesting that you fill it in in duplicate; please then send it back to us within 3 days of the above postal date.

To this end, a pre-paid envelope has been included.

The Chancellor
L. van Vuuren

Increasing polarisation

From the start of the war, the number of university registrations declined rapidly. In the academic year 1942-1943, the German occupier had set a half year labour conscription for all upcoming students so that new first year students could not start their studies until around Christmas. Among other things, this made studying clandestinely very popular at the time.

Students who no longer wished to be registered with the university, or could not be, were privately supported in their studies by some of the professors. In the years that followed, this form of studying increased, particularly when many students absconded in the latter phases of the war.

Late in 1942 and early 1943, the situation became grimmer. On the war fronts, the advance of the *Wehrmacht* was stopped, the German Sixth Army capitulated at Stalingrad, and the Third Reich's fortunes seemed to have turned. A huge Allied army gathered on the other side of the North Sea and the bombing offensive by the US Ninth Air Force and British Royal Air Force began. In the Netherlands, violent resistance now got off the ground.

Things became restless at the universities, too. Late in 1942, rumours circulated that a massive deportation of students for the *Arbeitseinsatz* (forced labour deployment by the Nazis) was underway. In December 1942, an attempt was made in Utrecht to set fire to the university's administration, the aim of which was to make the apprehension of students who refused the forced labour deployment difficult. Opinion regarding the success of this action was divided. De Moulin spoke of the total destruction of the administration's files, but it was also rumoured that the damage was scarcely perceptible. Nevertheless, that information had been lost is clear from the fact that the university called all students to send their personal data. De Moulin's Council of Representatives responded to the rumours about deportation with a call to strike. University chancellor Van Vuuren thus saw no other alternative than to have the Christmas holiday begin early once again.

In January 1943, following the events of the previous month, Van Vuuren indicated that he wished to get in touch with the illegal student movement. De Moulin, as the Board's local representative, had a number of conversations with the rector. In these, the rector made it clear that he wanted the students to stop their illegal activities.

Moreover, he wanted them to work with the university's administration to ensure that the Dutch university's community and culture were not lost. Ultimately, this conversation led nowhere. In De Moulin's own words: 'The demands made by Mr R.M. [Rector Magnificus] … which include that we cease our activities and completely surrender ourselves to his leadership are rejected by us as totally unacceptable.' Years later, after the war, De Moulin would view the rector's stance as one resulting from the difficult position in which he found himself. He recalled the words with which Van Vuuren had said farewell that night: 'Perhaps we do mean the same thing.'

Meanwhile, the contacts between the student resistance movement and other resistance bodies were tightened. In a report from 1943, De Moulin mentions an advisor from a 'higher coordinating body in the resistance.' Nothing is known either about the identity or about the practical role this person played.

Declaration of Loyalty

The Christmas holiday came to an end in February 1943 and the Council of Representatives repealed their call for a strike. However, vigilance remained necessary. Then, on 5 February 1943, General Seyffardt, Commander of the Waffen SS Dutch Volunteer Legion was liquidated by the resistance. As a matter of reprisal, the Germans arrested 600 students from Amsterdam, Delft, Utrecht and Wageningen and transferred them to Vught concentration camp. Three days later, a further 1,200 students were arrested. Education was suspended immediately in various cities. The Council of Nine advised students to lay down all activities and the board of Utrecht University closed the university.

Having the university shut down was undesirable for the authorities. However, continuing on as one had done before was also no longer possible: the NSB in particular intimated that studying should be seen as a favour one was granted, which could only be bestowed upon young people with certain intellectual and ideological qualities. Moreover, one had to prevent the German authorities at some point from getting fed up with the unruly students and closing the Dutch universities altogether. In order to ensure a more reliable student population, Professor Van Dam, Secretary General to the Department of Education, Science and Protection of Culture, desired loyalty from the students.

As a condition for permission to study, students were obliged to sign a Declaration of Loyalty:

The undersigned ... herewith solemnly declares that he will conscientiously and in good faith comply with the applicable laws, regulations and other ordinations in the Dutch occupied territories and that he will refrain from any actions directed against the German Reich, the German Wehrmacht or the Dutch authorities, or from any proceeding that, given the prevailing circumstances, may endanger public order at the establishments of higher education.

Ondergeteekende

geboren   te

wonende

verklaart hiermede plechtig, dat hij de in het bezette Neder-landsche gebied geldende wetten, verordeningen en andere beschikkingen naar eer en geweten zal nakomen en zich zal onthouden van iedere tegen het Duitsche Rijk, de Duitsche weermacht, of de Nederlandsche autoriteiten gerichte handeling, zoomede van handelingen of gedragingen welke de openbare orde aan de inrichtingen van hooger onderwijs, gezien de vigeerende omstandigheden, in gevaar brengen.

7180 · 3 · 6 · '43 · K 983

Declaration of Loyalty

On 6 March 1943, the national Council of Nine called on the students to refuse to sign the Declaration of Loyalty, to refuse to allow themselves to be employed in Germany and, for the duration of the war, to refuse to take part in any education. On 13 March, the official message regarding the Declaration of Loyalty was published. Students were given until 10 April to sign the declaration. On the tenth, the Domplein - the central square in Utrecht - was filled with supporters and opponents alike. People tried in every way possible to persuade declaration signers not to succumb to the Germans. In the end, after the fierce dispute, actions taken by the Council of Representatives and intensive involvement by De Moulin, only 12,6 per cent of the Utrecht students signed the declaration. This fiasco led the occupying forces to focus more on recruiting labour. A university populated by law-abiding students and teachers proved to be an illusion. The threat of conscription into the *Arbeitseinsatz* and reprisals against parents hung in the air. Arrests among those in the student resistance started to take place more regularly. The result was that resistance in the form it had taken until then, ended.

The situation in which De Moulin now found himself became very threatening indeed. Partly because of his illegal work, the arrests that had taken place in his immediate surroundings and the deteriorating situation in the Netherlands (which later became apparent during the strikes of April and May 1943), he decided to leave the occupied Netherlands.

In previous years, he had already mapped out a possible escape route and had prepared himself, along with year club comrades Lodewijk Parren and Armand Berg. Already in 1942, a boat lay ready in Zaltbommel to sail to England. Unfortunately, the men could not obtain enough fuel to execute their plan. Furthermore, due to measures taken by the Germans, fleeing by boat had become near to impossible and the trip across the Channel was very dangerous.

Daan and Lodewijk therefore decided to try a different route and attempt to reach London by way of Belgium, France and Spain. Armand, as well as De Moulin's younger brother Peter, followed soon afterwards. Once they had arrived in England, they wanted to devote themselves to assisting the Allies. Or, as Daan and Lodewijk wrote later, 'The undersigned regarded their work in the Netherlands to have ended and have left the country in order to make themselves available to Her Majesty's Government.'

Chapter 2

Journey to England

Although he was fully aware of the consequences, Daniël de Moulin refused to sign the Declaration of Loyalty. Because this refusal meant he would be deported under the Nazi *Arbeitseinsatz* he had two alternatives: 'go underground or leave and join the Allies'. Many people in the Netherlands, like him, faced this same dilemma.

Dissatisfaction and the politics of occupation

Many of the 2,000 or so Dutch who, like De Moulin and Parren, escaped to England, also indicated that their main motive for doing so was a patriotic one. They left for 'queen and country' and in order to be able 'to contribute to the good cause'. Their main objection to remaining in the country was, of course, the German occupation. However, specific measures taken by the occupying forces were often what induced people to leave. Little by little, the Germans sought to employ the Dutch economy to serve the German war effort and to make Dutch public life more pro-German. The *Arbeitseinsatz* is probably the best-known example of this. From 1943 onwards, an increasing number of young men were called up to supplement the shortage of manpower in the many German factories. Besides students, those enlisted for this service were primarily workers, reserve officers and conscripts. Professional officers had already preceded them in 1942. So, an important incentive for taking the plunge and go to England, or for going underground, was to escape measures like the *Arbeitseinsatz*.

In addition to the measures taken by the Germans to annex the Dutch economy, there were numerous other regulations imposed upon the Dutch. According to the Germans, the Dutch were also a master race and therefore the Germans wanted to win them over to

Der Höhere SS- und Polizeiführer
beim Reichskommissar für die besetzten
niederländischen Gebiete DdS - III C -
Dr. Nr. 2896/43 -   Den Haag, den   28   Mai 1943.

AUFFORDERUNG.

Es wurde festgestellt, dass der Student ..D.d..Moulin..
.... der Anordnung
Nr. 55/43 vom 4.5.43 nicht Folge leistete und zur Meldung am
6.5.43 nicht erschien.- Da er bis zur Stunde in dem Lager Ommen
noch nicht eingerückt ist, werden Sie als Inhaber der elter -
lichen Gewalt oder Vormund gefragt, was Sie für die pflichtgemässe
Meldung Ihres Sohnes veranlasst hatten und was Sie im Hinblick
auf Stück IV/4 der Anordnung Nr. 55/43 tun werden.

Der Höhere SS- und Polizeiführer
beim Reichskommissar für die besetzten
niederländischen Gebiete
gez. R a u t e r
SS-Gruppenführer und Generalleutnant
der Polizei.

F.d.R. .... (Licentgrad).

OPROEP.

Vastgesteld werd, dat de student...D de Moulin........
....geen gehoor gaf
aan de beschikking Nr. 55/43 van de 4.5.43 en bij de melding op
de 6.5.43 niet verschoon. Daar hij tot op dit oogenblik niet in
het kamp Ommen aangekomen is, wordt U als uitoefenaar van het
ouderlijke gezag of voogdij gevraagd, welke maatregelen gij ge-
nomen hebt, ten aanzien van de verplichte melding van Uw zoon
en wat U met het oog op stuk IV/4 der beschikking Nr.55/43 van de
4.5.43 zult doen.

Der Höhere SS- und Polizeiführer
beim Reichskommissar für die besetzten
niederländischen Gebiete
gez. R a u t e r
SS-Gruppenführer und Generalleutnant der
Polizei.

Appeal written to De Moulin's parents by the German authorities after De Moulin failed to report for forced labour; by this time, he had already departed for England. The translation is given below.

Appeal
Student D de Moulin *has been found not to have complied with decision No. 55/43 of 4 May 1943 and did not report on 6 May 1943. Because he has not arrived at camp Ommen to date, you, who exercise parental authority or function as custodian, are being asked what measures you have taken regarding your son's mandatory appearance and what, in view of part IV/4 of the decision No. 55/43 dated 4 May 1943 you will do about it.*

Chief of the SS & Police of the Netherlands
Rauter
SS-Obergruppenführer [senior group leader] *and General of Police*

Small demonstration of opposition by De Moulin. The original sign reads: 'Maartensdijk: Jews not welcome'. It was changed to: 'Maartensdijk: NSB (National Socialist Movement) not welcome'.

national socialism, as well as to remove the Jews from Dutch society. In November 1940, Jewish civil servants were laid off and shortly afterwards, all public places were declared forbidden territory for them. From May 1942 onwards, Jews were required to wear a Star of David clearly visible on their jackets and less than three months later, the deportations to concentration camps began.

The Germans carried out their operations gradually so that only a small portion of the population was affected each time. As a result, mass public protests against the German-imposed regulations remained limited for a long time. Even so, the measures created a latent anti-German sentiment among many of the Dutch. Newly-introduced measures, such as the Declaration of Loyalty for students, further served to fuel their aversion and often determined the moment of their resistance or departure.

Going underground or emigrating

One means of evading the German measures was by going into hiding. However, for many this was not an option: it was difficult to come by a reliable hiding place and it was extremely dangerous for both the person in hiding as well as the hosts, because if caught, they could be sentenced to death. Moreover, the thought of staying in a stuffy attic or cramped basement not knowing just how long the war would last, was not attractive.

Escaping to a non-occupied country as an alternative to going underground had its own limitations. For most of the Dutch, bound as they were by work or family, lacking knowledge of other countries and deterred by the penalties in force, England remained a pipe dream. Without a hiding place or escape route, they did their best to just get on with their lives.

A small number of Dutch did leave. Their departure was not so much a flight as it was 'an act of defiance and a refusal to be used by the Germans', says Agnes Dessing in her dissertation entitled *Tulpen voor Wilhelmina* (*Tulips for Wilhelmina*, Queen of the Netherlands from 1890 – 1948). The decision to leave raised many practical questions: who to trust? Was there someone, perhaps, who could provide help? Should we go alone, or together? What route should we take? Should we go straight to London by way of the North Sea (a journey by sea of several hundred kilometres), or head south through occupied Europe via Portugal (a journey by land of thousands of kilometres across the occupied territories of Belgium and France and German-friendly Spain)?

The North Sea

A sea crossing to London – a distance of 340 kilometres (212 miles) as the crow flies – appeared to be an attractive and logical route for escaping to England. The distance was short; it was 'just' a matter of getting across undetected. The flat Dutch coast was an ideal starting point and with a little luck, one could make the crossing in a couple of days. Essential to this were a good (preferably seaworthy) boat, fuel, food and adequate marine equipment. That in turn required good – but even more important – trustworthy connections; betrayal was a great risk. A further, not to be underestimated, peril was the sea itself. Depending upon weather conditions, the trip could take up to a week.

The North Sea route was used primarily in the first two years after the German invasion. After that, its popularity rapidly declined. The beach and dunes became inaccessible as German lookouts were posted along the coast, and the area itself was patrolled both from the air and on the water. When the construction of the *Atlantikwall* began in 1942 (an extensive system of coastal fortifications built by Nazi Germany as a defense against an Allied invasion), surveillance was further tightened and the entire coastline became a *Sperrgebiet* (restricted area). Also, an increasing number of German regulations were imposed which hampered an escape attempt over the water. From 1941 onwards, possession of a boat or an outboard motor was not possible without a permit. A year later, such ownership was banned altogether and all boats and engines were seized. Both professional and recreational boating were restricted and being on the water was only allowed in very exceptional cases. In addition, there was a critical shortage of fuel. A trip by sea consequently became next to impossible.

The name '*Engelandvaarder*' (literally translated as 'England farer') to designate those who escaped to England during the Second World War to join the Allied forces by way of the North Sea, originated from this fact. However, only a small number of *Engelandvaarders* actually emigrated to England via this route. It was a dangerous passage and less than a quarter of the attempts were successful. Out of a total 1,706 successful *Engelandvaarders* that Agnes Dessing was able to trace, only 172 reached England by way of the North Sea.

Engelandvaarders on their way to England in a canoe.

Sweden

A second route to England ran through Sweden. This northern escape route was used primarily by sailors, who signed on with a ship and then deserted in neutral Sweden. They simply got off the boat and did not come back. If the boat did not moor in Sweden and the captain forbade them from going ashore, then a lifeboat could provide the solution; alternatively, the sailors swam the last leg of the trip to Sweden.

The Germans were well aware of the fact that more sailors left with the ship than returned home and they took measures to prevent desertion. As of March 1941, passengers had to be in possession of a pre-war seaman's book as evidence that they were not 'opportunistic' members of the merchant navy. Moreover, the captain was held responsible for his crew and the Germans threatened reprisals against relatives of sailors who deserted. All in all, this greatly dampened the enthusiasm for deserting.

The northern route was nevertheless very popular. In the second year of the war, several dozen Dutch sailors succeeded in reaching Sweden. From 1943 onwards, there was a huge shortage of sailors and it once again became easier to sign on with a ship without a seaman's book. For this reason, in the autumn of 1943 the number of *Engelandvaarders* in Sweden increased by 200, as a result of which a colony of a couple of hundred Dutch people and many other foreigners was formed. For them the challenge was to get to England to join the Dutch forces. At the start of the war, this was still possible via Russia, Japan and Canada, but after the German invasion of Russia this route became impossible and England could only be reached by air. Even so, for most a quick passage by air was not possible. Occasionally British bombers would fly between Sweden and England and they were often loaded with mail. They could therefore only take a handful of people with them each time they flew. Furthermore, it was an unpleasant flight. In order to avoid enemy fire and fighter aircraft, the British flew as high as they could over German-occupied Norway; so, the *Engelandvaarders* had to sit between the mail and a bomb hatch for five hours in thin, freezing air.

Because the *Engelandvaarders* could only push in piecemeal, long waiting lists formed. The many refugees had to make themselves useful prior to their departure and were deployed as lumberjacks in the forests of northern Sweden. This was a considerable disappointment to the men who had not come to harvest trees. Devoid of any entertainment, they braved swarms of mosquitoes in summer, intense cold in the winter and lice in the barracks in all the seasons. Far away from civilization, it was a difficult and monotonous existence. It was not

Engelandvaarders in Sweden.

until a special office for Dutch refugees was opened in Stockholm in 1943 that the situation improved for the stranded *Engelandvaarders*. Their monthly payments rose and they were moved to camps nearer to the cities so that they could take leave. Nevertheless, getting to England remained a big problem.

This problem was not resolved until the Americans started to fly their stranded aircrew to England in the summer of 1944. There was enough room for the Dutch in the American bombers and after an average waiting time of about a year, their final voyage got underway. A total of 528 *Engelandvaarders* reached their final destination by way of Sweden. Of these, more than 70 per cent had a seafaring background.

The south

The southern and longest route to England ran through Belgium and France via Switzerland or Spain to Portugal. Thousands of kilometres had to be travelled and the duration of the trip ranged from several days to as much as two years. It was a route with many dangers, but at the same time it was the route with the highest chance of success and chosen by most *Engelandvaarders*. The greatest peril of the trip lay in the border controls. If you wanted to travel abroad after 1940, then you not only had to have a passport, but also an identity card and a holiday card. As holiday cards were not issued to just anyone, crossing the border illegally was inevitable. Those caught taking part in '*Unerlaubte Ausreise*' (unauthorized departure) risked imprisonment or a fine. However, if the Germans discovered that you had not only crossed the border illegally but were also planning to travel to England, the indictment was '*Feindbegünstigung*' (treason). This was a very serious offense; if convicted, life imprisonment or the death penalty were the result.

Acquiring the right currency also proved very difficult without all the official papers. In order to change money a travel permit was required, it was therefore important to either obtain forged papers or to exchange money illegally.

Due to the many controls, travelling by public transport was risky. At the same time, it was attractive because of the long distances that could be covered quickly compared to, for example, walking. Controls could be avoided by not staying on the train until the last stop, or by getting off the train on the wrong side. Besides, the French and Belgian railway and customs officials were generally favorably disposed to the *Engelandvaarders* and they often offered them a helping hand.

The most commonly used route ran from the Dutch border via Antwerp and Brussels. From Brussels, it ran to Paris or eastwards to Switzerland.

Switzerland was a neutral enclave moving between the Allies and Germany and it was not looking to welcome these refugees with open arms. The Swiss border was heavily guarded and, initially, the authorities only allowed soldiers of the Allied countries to cross the border. These men fell into the category of 'escaped Allied prisoners of war'. Moreover, because they were financially supported by the Dutch Government, it was especially attractive for the Swiss to shelter the Dutch soldiers. Everyone else had to penetrate deep into Switzerland because those who were arrested less than 12 kilometres from the border risked being sent back. If one did succeed in getting into Switzerland, a long wait for transit papers, enabling you to travel via Vichy France (the southern unoccupied part of France), Spain and Portugal to England, awaited you. As of 1942, due to German pressure and the elimination of the demarcation line (the boundary between occupied and unoccupied France), travel by this route had become impossible. The only option left was to leave safe Switzerland

The Swiss Camp for Dutchmen in Cossonay.

by illegally crossing the border again and continuing on via France, Spain and Portugal to England.

Engelandvaarders who travelled to Paris arrived in a vibrant city with bustling streets and crowded cafés, which offered them ample opportunity to blend in with the crowd. However, finding accommodation was a major problem. Hotels were required to keep guest lists which were checked by the Germans. Although, some hotels did welcome unregistered guests on the condition that they left the hotel by around 6 am, before the German controls began. Many *Engelandvaarders* lingered a while in or around Paris. Many Dutch farms could be found in the area around the French capital. They had originated decades earlier and grateful use was made of them for rest and socializing, in exchange for labour. The food was good and the risk of getting caught was low; on occasion even, someone would change their plans and simply remain in this comfortable spot.

The majority, however, moved south to the border with Spain. Here the toughest part of their journey awaited them: a dangerous trek through the Pyrenees. The Pyrenees were desolate and inhospitable mountains, with peaks of over 3,000 metres. They were poetically called 'les montagnes de la peur et de l'espérance' (the mountains of fear and hope) after the fear of the difficult journey and the hope of freedom. Accompanied by a local guide (often smugglers), the *Engelandvaarders* – who were generally highly inexperienced and lacked mountain equipment – trekked through the mountains at breakneck speed to evade German dog patrols.

After climbing up and down for a few days, they arrived in free Spain. However, the welcoming reception consisted primarily of an immediate arrest by the *Guardia Civil*, the Spanish police. After a brief interrogation, the detainees were transferred to a prison in one of the larger cities, or to the concentration camp at Miranda de Ebro.

Although they were neutral, Spain under Franco had a moderately pro-German regime and it was not particularly sympathetic to the *Engelandvaarders*. Detention could last for months. Once freed, the refugees were still stuck in Madrid for a long time because neither the Spanish nor the Portuguese authorities applied for the necessary travel documents wholeheartedly. Like Franco, the Portuguese dictator Salazar was *deutschfreundlich* (German-friendly). To be allowed transit to Portugal, both a visa for the next destination and a Spanish

Engelandvaarders in the Pyrenees, January 1944.

The concentration camp at Miranda de Ebro.

exit visa were required. However, in order to obtain a Spanish exit visa, a Portuguese entry visa was needed. The wrangling could take months and all that time, the *Engelandvaarders* were stuck in Madrid. Not until 1943, when the fortunes of war turned against Germany, did Spain and Portugal become more cooperative.

Once in Portugal, the *Engelandvaarders* went to Praia das Maçãs, a coastal town west of Lisbon, where they were given shelter prior to their transit to England. In the meantime, they had to prepare a detailed description of themselves and their intended journey. In advance of a possible Channel crossing, these descriptions, as well as the results of a medical examination, were dispatched to England where they could be checked for their credibility and reliability. In principle, only young men of military age who were useful to the Allied war effort were given approval to make the trip. The others were only authorized to travel if a job had been arranged for them in England or elsewhere.

Until their departure for England, the Dutch government provided the *Engelandvaarders* with room and board, pocket money and clothing. Although this was, in principle, perceived to be ideal, the long wait and money wasting was soon felt to be highly frustrating. After a perilous journey and an often long period of captivity in Spain, the *Engelandvaarders* were once again twiddling their thumbs.

On average, the *Engelandvaarders* needed fifteen months to reach England by way of the southern route. The time this took was so long not only because of the distance, but also because of the many delays along the way. Some *Engelandvaarders* hung around in Paris, were imprisoned in Spain, had no more money or could not continue their journey for other reasons. Even so, nearly 60 per cent of the *Engelandvaarders* identified by Dessing travelled by way of the southern route; this was a total of 985 people, including 358 who travelled via Switzerland.

Failed attempts

As far as we know, around 2,000 people undertook a successful trip to England, of which at least 48 were women. However, unfortunate circumstances or betrayal ensured that many attempts failed.

Some of the *Engelandvaarders* (185) had already attempted a journey to England before their crossing was successful. There were also those whose attempts were stranded and who refrained from trying a second time. Their boats were discovered or sank; they got stuck halfway or they returned home disillusioned. Some aspiring *Engelandvaarders* came very close but were arrested en route. Some were allowed to return home, but many were captured and taken away. They spent the rest of the war in captivity, were executed or died in the camps. Finally, there was a group that left but from whom nothing more was ever heard again.

Needless to say, *Engelandvaarders* did not flaunt the fact that they were planning to leave for England. In the known cases of failed attempts, we only know someone left for England thanks to, for example, that one trusted friend who was informed. Many drowned in the North Sea, got lost in the Pyrenees or were arrested. We will never know what happened on their way. At least 598 *Engelandvaarders* were stranded. Of these, 233 were able to talk about their attempts; 236 did not survive. The fates of the rest remain unknown.

England

The *Engelandvaarders* who arrived safely in England – whether by sea or by air – were detained by the British security service MI5 and taken away to an old school complex: the Royal Victoria Patriotic Asylum for the Orphan Daughters of Soldiers killed in the Crimean War, or the Patriotic School for short. Here, completely cut off from the outside world, all of the *Engelandvaarders* were interrogated and investigated for their political reliability in order to unmask any German spies. The complete story of their journey to England, written while in Portugal, was reviewed: place names, contact persons, and routes were repeatedly and painstakingly checked, verified and compared to what the British already knew about those who had crossed over. The slightest deviation in the story led to intensified and prolonged interrogations, long enough to learn whether or not the *Engelandvaarder* was reliable. The *Engelandvaarder* was also asked to provide military information which might be relevant to the Allies for future invasions, such as artillery deployments, where the *Feldkommandantur* (Field commandant) was located in a village or town, and what units belonged to a particular garrison.

If the *Engelandvaarder* was approved, he or she was briefly a free person, after which he was once again secured, this time by the Dutch intelligence service (the so-called Police Field Service). This service duplicated the British investigation and also asked the *Engelandvaarder* about living conditions in the occupied Netherlands and for names of harmful countrymen for the benefit of post-war justice. Those *Engelandvaarders* who were also approved by this intelligence service could finally enter England to serve in the Allied armies.

De Moulin: Go underground or leave?

Because De Moulin thought it would have 'been practically impossible, for example, to be shut in a room for a year' and because he ran the risk of being arrested and unmasked as an important person in the Utrecht student resistance movement, he decided to risk the journey to England. Bound by neither work nor family and just 23 years old, he had the ideal profile for an *Engelandvaarder*.

He and his friends, Lodewijk Parren and Armand Berg, had already prepared for the crossing in 1942. They wanted to attempt to reach England by way of the North Sea with a boat that lay waiting in the city of Zaltbommel; but the plan failed due to a lack of fuel. Therefore, on 3 May 1943, when he thought he had a reliable route to England, De Moulin (24) - together with his best friend Lodewijk Parren (24) and Lodewijk's girlfriend Rolande Kloesmeijer (Kloesje, 19) - left from Utrecht and travelled south.

Chapter 3

Chronicle of the adventures of Daniël de Moulin during his trip to England in 1943

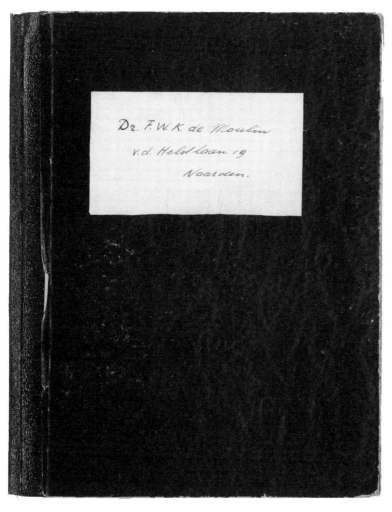

Cover of the chronicle, addressed to Daniël's parents.

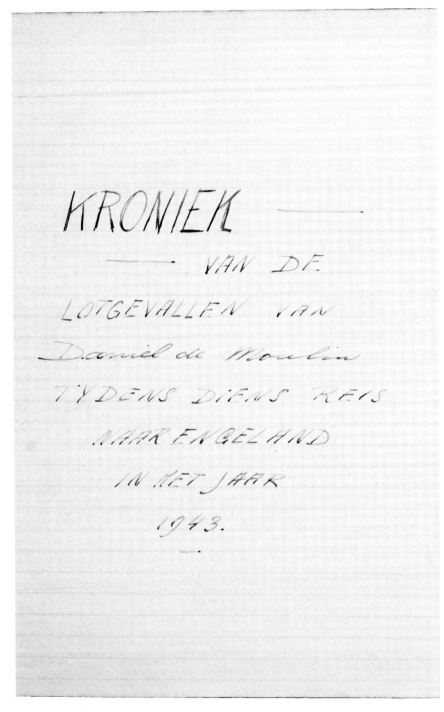

KRONIEK

— . VAN DE
LOTGEVALLEN VAN
Daniël de Moulin
TYDENS DIENS REIS
NAAR ENGELAND
IN HET JAAR
1943.

The chronicle's title page.

2/L

VOORWOORD

Dit geschrift beoogt een weernis te
zijn van mijn lotgevallen gedurende
mijn tocht van Nederland naar
Engeland, van 3 Mei tot 27 October
1943.

Litteraire schoonheid zal men er
niet in aantreffen, ik heb alleen
onze lotgevallen voor jullie, mij
lieve ouders, willen vertellen en
jullie zult mij de vele taalfouten
die het bevat niet kwalijk
nemen.

Daar het alleen voor jullie is, wil
ik onder geen voorwaarde dat
het uitgeleend wordt aan anderen
dan de onmiddellijke familie.
Lodewijk, die jullie dit boek te
hand zal stellen, zal het wel
willen aanvullen met monde-
linge verhalen.

Het is de moeilijkste periode van
mijn leven geweest, ik ben er ...
... gekomen en heb hierdoor
... van ervaringen opgedaan
die mij voor mijn ... leven, dat
ik ... tegemoet ga, van
grote waarde zullen zijn.

The chronicle's foreword.

Foreword

This document is intended to be a record of my adventures during the journey from the Netherlands to England, from 3 May to 27 October 1943. One will not find literary beauty; I sought only to tell these adventures to you, my dear parents [Frederik and Albertina de Moulin], and you shall therefore not hold against me the many language errors it contains. As it is meant for you only, under no circumstances do I want you to lend it out to any one other than those from our immediate family. Lodewijk, who will hand this book over to you, will likely supplement its content with his stories.

It has been the most difficult period of my life; I got through it and as a result, gained a wealth of experience that will be of great value to me for the rest of my life, which I look forward to with great confidence.

Lodewijk's farewell letter to his parents.

Dear Mum and Dad,

I am writing you this letter with an unwilling pen and a pounding heart.

I have thought about it for a long time, long before this, and I always hoped it would not be necessary, but now for the first time, the problem has become acute. And despite how very difficult it is, I have made a decision. I am making a radical move. I will not go into slavery voluntarily. My call-up to enlist has not yet arrived, but waiting any longer would only make things more difficult. I am leaving this country and I have an opportunity. I know what this means for both of you. I am jeopardizing everything that you have given to me with great difficulty and care.

But I have no choice. Mum, Dad, forgive me. I could have talked to you about it. But the result would have been the same and this farewell seemed better to me. I told [my brother] Henk but other than him, no one else knows.

Tell no one. Many accommodating minds could throw a spanner in the works and thereby make my journey difficult, if not impossible. It is truly better not to mourn and not to look for me. The deliverer of this letter knows nothing.

Dear folks, I can write no more. Have courage and we will get through this.

Much love from your loving eldest.

Wiek

PS I have made an inventory of my junk. Henk knows all about it.

Again, it is best to talk to absolutely no one about this. The police and others are watchful.

Nobody can change anything for the better.

Hugs

Lieve Moeder en Vader

Met een onwillige pen en een kloppend hard schrijf ik U deze brief. Veel heb ik erover gedacht, reeds lang voor dezen en steeds hoopte ik dat het niet nodig zou zijn, maar eerst nu werd het probleem acuut. En ik heb gekozen, hoe zwaar ook. Ik neem de radicale weg. En vrijwillig ga ik mee in slavernij. Mijn oproep is er nog niet, maar langer wachten zou de zaak maar moeilijker maken. Ik ga weg uit dit landen ik heb een kans. Ik weet wat dit voor U beiden beteekent. Alles wat U mij met veel moeite en zorgen gegeven hebt zet u op het spel maar ik kan niet anders doen. Moeder, vader vergeef mij. Ik had er met U over kunnen praten. Het resultaat zou hetzelfde geweest zijn en dit afscheid viel mij beter. Slechts heb ik het verteld, verder weet niemand meer.

Verzwijg het voor de buitenwereld. Veiligheidsdiensten zouden er iets van kunnen gooien en daardoor mijn reis verzwaren, ze niet onmogelijk maken. Het is werkelijk beter om niet te penzen en

Introduction

Although perhaps superfluously, I would like to mention the reasons that led to me to leave the Netherlands; a step which was to have far greater consequences than I ever could have imagined at the time and which may give my life a completely different turn.

As you know, I was very active in work for the resistance for a good two years, especially in the student movement. When in March it was announced that the infamous Declaration of Loyalty had to be signed, we knew that we would not do so. However, we also knew that the Germans would react vigorously and rapidly, probably in the form of a deportation to Germany, a suspicion that has since proven to be correct.

As I was not prepared, under any conditions, to surrender myself, only two alternatives therefore remained: either go into hiding, or leave to join the Allies. Had I opted for the first alternative, I could have done nothing further and would moreover have run the risk of getting caught in the long run, as there was no telling how long the war would last.

Had I been caught as a student in hiding, then the role I had recently played in the resistance would have come to light. Then, without question, the death penalty would have followed, because, in the eyes of the Germans, I was not just once but many times over guilty and deserving of death. In addition to these substantive reasons for departure, I should add that, mentally, it would have been near to impossible for me to have remained stowed away in a small room for a whole year.

On the other hand, if I was caught in Belgium or France then the only offence I would have been guilty of was that I was residing in that country illegally. The penalty for this was that I would have been obliged to work in Germany, a far better option. If I succeeded in getting to England, then I could openly and wholly commit myself to the good cause, although I never intended to go and fight because if there is anything I have learned from all of this, it is that I have a fundamental abhorrence for anything military.

Ultimately, I was of the opinion that we had a good route and so, after careful consideration and much inner struggle, I decided to go. It was not easy, the worst part being that I had to leave without saying farewell to you. However, I wanted to spare you this. Had all gone well, then after one week you would have received a letter from me through Peter de Moulin and I would, as I thought, have reached Spain. But as I will tell you in the following pages, things turned out differently, and even though they ultimately ended well, they often did so in such unexpected ways that I have no doubt providence had a hand in it.

Preparations

When in March [1943] it became clear that all would soon go amiss, we began the preparations. The main concern was the route. Kloesje had repeatedly related something about "subordinates" who, through instructions issued by her organization, had arrived in England in a very short time. So it is understandable that I turned to her for this. She surprised me by saying that she too had to leave. The Gestapo (German Secret State Police) had urged her to leave within a specified time, otherwise she would be arrested. So if I agreed to go with her, she would ensure a route. It was unfortunate that she had broken contact with her organization, but she knew other ways to get information.

Kloesje - Rolande Kloesmeijer

Then we discussed the desirability of taking someone else with us, and we both thought of Lodewijk. Lodewijk and Kloesje were then "engaged", but never in my life have I seen a more remarkable engagement. Nobody could know, not even me. To this day I still do not understand why I did not suspect anything at all, but that may be because I was too busy to pay attention to such things.

I knew that it was a risky business leaving the planning of the journey to Kloesje, when I thought back to the sleepover at the Veluwe. But after I had a serious talk with her and emphasized that this was a life or death situation, and she seemed to understand, I left the matter to her. Moreover, the benefit of travelling with a girl is that one is less noticeable. Besides this, according to her she spoke fluent French. This, added to the fact that I still believed that she was a first-class spy and therefore incredibly smart, and the fact that I did not wish to leave her alone in Holland only to become prey to the prying eyes of the Gestapo, or be left in other such creepy settings, resulted in us taking her along. Lodewijk naturally had another motive! When approached, Lodewijk immediately agreed.

Cheerful, we walked to the Broese [bookshop] and bought a guidebook for the south of France and the Pyrenees and a book for learning Spanish in seven lessons.

While Kloesje went to work, I spent my free time studying Spanish so that when we finally descended the Pyrenees, I noticed that I could, to my own satisfaction, understand and make myself understood in the language, although misunderstandings were inevitable! Lodewijk was responsible for our physical care and again and again came running in happily with 5-pound tins of butter and kilos of tea so that we had eventually stored enough provisions in my room to supply a warship. We also went out scouting for *obati* so that we left with more than enough medicine. By some strange coincidence, a large part of our stock consisted of nerve-relieving remedies!

We also made sure our personal equipment, clothes and, in particular, shoes were in order. Kloesje went about this by ordering suits that were not ready on time and by instructing a variety of friends to take care of the rest, including having her shoes resoled. You can imagine her outrage when, on the day of departure, nothing proved to be in order! She therefore left with shoes that scarcely had soles. As a result she experienced the "pleasure" we had predicted these shoes would bring her during the journey.

By diligently saving, selling and pawning some things off, including my Winkler Prins Encyclopedia to Hans Rijsbosch, and my microscope to the dentist, Krijn Soeteman, we eventually obtained a total of 400 guilders. Everything took place with the utmost secrecy so that when we finally announced our departure to a few intimate friends, it was like a bolt out of the blue. Kloesje took many trips, diligently recorded addresses and came up with all sorts of sketch drawings of border crossings and the like. We were to be transferred over the Belgian border by a personal friend of hers.

And thus I left Utrecht on the morning of 3 May, escorted by Wim Heirsch and Armand Berg. Wim hastily gave me the address of family of his in Brussels, which proved to be of untold value to us. I was to meet Kloesje in [the city of] Den Bosch and Lodewijk in Roosendaal. It was no jolly affair this leave-taking from Utrecht where I had so many memories. But the same feeling of irrationally knowing, which I could not really describe and that felt inevitable, also helped me to get over this.

Belgian border, or the first argument

In a small pub somewhere in Roosendaal, three people sat at a table looking at each other angrily. The reason was that Kloesje's friend had not shown up at the appointed hour. To make matters worse, the pub's proprietor, as an anecdote, told us that in the past week the border had been so heavily guarded by great swarms of [Dutch fascist] NSB police that even professional smugglers did not dare cross it. In order to kill time, Lodewijk started to insult Kloesje; he thought her friend should have been there on time and blamed her for not knowing that the border was so firmly closed. We finally just left and headed south haphazardly. After five minutes, whilst cursing one another, we asserted we did not plan to have ourselves shot just to please the other two. We turned around and went back to the pub angrily, where by then, Kloesje's friend had arrived. He was an ugly sort of Belgian but very friendly and he helped us tremendously.

Outside the pub stood a lorry; a closed truck into which we were loaded. This rattling and jolting thing took us to another pub not far from the border. The romance of the French Revolution came to life for us, although looking back, I seriously doubt that the Scarlet

Pimpernel appreciated his adventures to the extent he would have us believe. All kinds of smugglers, murderers and other gentlemen sat in the pub when we entered and they pityingly shook their heads when they heard that we wanted to cross the border. We felt really anxious and could empathize with how Napoleon felt at Smolensk: 'Move forward or go back?!' We decided to move on.

So the three of us walked along a back road pointed out to us, to a small village through which the border ran. There we were met by Kloesje's friend, who pushed us into one of the cottages there. The street in front was Belgian, the house itself was on Dutch territory. There we exchanged our Dutch money into francs, of course at black market prices, meaning that we lost a lot of money.

A barbed wire barricade ran straight through the village. For convenience's sake, the villagers had made a big hole in it and when the police patrol was over, we crawled through it into Belgium where we were welcomed by a young girl, a smuggler's daughter, whose husband had recently died in the pursuit of that honourable profession. The girl led the way; I walked 100 metres behind her, and at the same distance behind me came Kloesje and Lodewijk, who covered the rear. We were taken through a few small villages where we were received with cheers and the exuberant joy of the villagers. We however, looking around for policemen and expecting to see Germans with the most bloodthirsty intentions behind every tree, could absolutely not see the fun in this. On a large asphalt road leading to the village where we had to board the train the following morning, the girl left us. By then, it was almost dark.

After ten minutes or so of walking, we saw a few Belgian gendarmes (policemen), walking towards us. We pulled guileless faces and acted very normally, but it is definitely not easy to pretend everything is normal when you are walking dressed in city clothes in a farming region, near a border and each with a large bag under your arm. So we were stopped and given the unexpected order to show 'Passports, please. But you probably don't have them so show us your Dutch identity papers.' We found it really humiliating to be caught so close to home and so we asked them if this could be avoided. In the end, after a long conversation, we managed to convince the gentlemen that we were going to work for relatives in France. They initially doubted this but a few packs of tobacco suddenly helped them to see the light. Then, the ice was broken and, cheerfully chatting with the gendarmes, we walked right up to the edge of the village after which they bid us a good trip and left. We all withdrew into the forest at the side of the road and made ourselves comfortable and slept contentedly.

Brussels

Awakened by the sun the next day, we ran to the station in the early hours of the morning. We arrived just in time. It was an early train for labourers to Antwerp.

We had an address in Antwerp, but as it was so early in the morning we decided to move on to Brussels. As a result, we did not make use of Kloesje's address in Antwerp, and fortunately so. It was to be quite an affair: we were to go to a place called Café des Sports and tell them we came from "the Chinese", after which we would receive all the assistance we needed immediately. Armand and two of his friends, who arrived a few days after us, did visit all the Cafés des Sports in Antwerp and announced that they had come from the Chinese. The responses to this varied greatly, from great hilarity to anxious inquiries as to their mental state. And the support they had expected to receive failed to materialize.

We arrived in Brussels without a hitch, only to notice that the trains in Brussels were just as crowded as those in Holland. Our reception by Wim's family was most hospitable. The family consisted of Wim's aunt and her husband, her daughter and husband, and two small children with a third on the way. The young lady was most charming and very beautiful, but her husband, who owned a photo shop, did not like us and the feeling was mutual. His wife resented the fact that he made us pay for a couple of passport photos he took of us and so did we. The young lady had a brother who often visited them and he was there when we arrived. I never imagined that our good Lord would disguise a divine emissary as a Belgian. Yet it was apparently so, for this man helped us enormously.

To begin with, he changed our money for us. Kloesje had thought it would be a good idea if we exchanged our money for German marks so that we could use it throughout occupied Europe, a plan we had welcomed enthusiastically. But unfortunately, when we arrived in Belgium with our pockets full of marks, they turned out to be of the kind which had no value outside of Germany and Holland. You see, there are two types of German bank notes: The '*Reichsbanknoten*' and

'*Reichskassescheine*'. One of the two types, the first I believe, was valid only in Germany and the Netherlands; the other was valid everywhere. Whatever the case may be, we of course had the sort which was not valid in Belgium or France. But by a blessed coincidence, the young man had a friend who was a banker who could exchange these notes clandestinely. Without a passport we could not exchange the money officially and besides, being in possession of these bank notes was illegal.

It also turned out that the young man was involved in secretly helping rich Jews get to Switzerland. For example, he brought the director [Heinz Littaur] of the Bijenkorf [department store] to Switzerland. According to the young man it was currently not possible to get into France. Some days earlier the Belgian-French border had been closed. Before that time, Belgians who could show their Belgian identity card could move freely into Northern France. But now it was forbidden to cross the border. Trains were searched from top to bottom and German troops made life miserable for those who were found in the border area. He therefore strongly advised us not to move onwards. Moreover, in France you also had something called the flying brigades who searched all trains, and around Paris there was a forbidden zone where you were not allowed to stay or travel without a permit. He advised us to stay in Belgium; he knew good hiding places. So there we were again; what should we do?!

After a fairly lengthy and eventful council of war, we decided to go anyway; the family we were staying with thought us to be completely mad. The next day, around twelve o'clock, we were met by a most charming young girl. She was the young man's fiancé and companion in many affairs, a truly brave and pleasant girl.

Having said our farewells to the compassionately head-shaking family, we climbed into the train that would take us via Dinant to a border town called Heer-Agimont. It was a very pleasant journey. The landscape in this region is magnificent; hilly and wooded with lovely villages and picturesque rivers. Having delivered us to a customs officer in Heer-Agimont, the young girl took leave of us and went back.

The French border

The customs officer lived with his wife and daughter in a shabby two-room house, where we were warmly welcomed and immediately offered cups of coffee and soup. The customs officer looked at us with great skepticism when he heard that we wanted to cross the border. According to him, this was not possible and he gave us countless reasons for not moving on. But because he used the language spoken in that region, which was a very strange kind of French, we did not understand him very well and so his argument was lost on us.

We left at nightfall. He took us near to the border where we could exchange our Belgian francs for French ones with, of course, the usual loss of 20 per cent. There, the customs officer left us saying that he thought it was too dangerous for him to continue, but not without extensively describing the road we should follow. The first French town was Givet, which is located on the tip of a sharp salient of France into Belgium, formed by the River Meuse. It looks something like this:

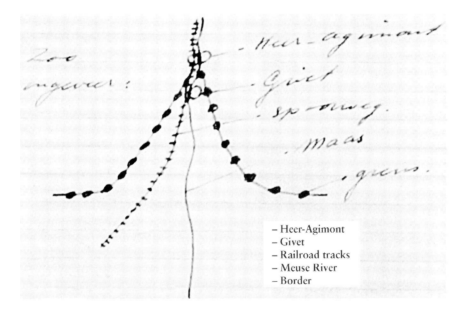

– Heer-Agimont
– Givet
– Railroad tracks
– Meuse River
– Border

It is an extremely narrow piece of France and therefore a most disadvantageous place to enter the country. It was almost dark when we walked through Givet; our arms locked together tightly so that we would not be noticed. Our luggage had been reduced to a briefcase for the three of us; we had left the rest in Brussels. We got through the town easily and ended up on the highway. When it got very dark, we did not dare go any further for fear of the patrols which, with an eye for smugglers, would increase both in number and in activity. Unfortunately, the area was not the best place to spend the night. Schematically, the situation was something like this:

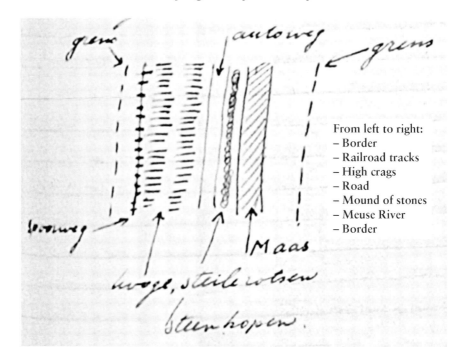

From left to right:
– Border
– Railroad tracks
– High crags
– Road
– Mound of stones
– Meuse River
– Border

To the right of the road were high crags and to the left a mound of stones and then the river. So we were virtually enclosed. The only thing we could do was to take cover amongst the stones. We found a hole where Kloesje and Lodewijk laid down and I laid flat on my stomach on a small hill on the lookout. Then began one of the most awful nights we experienced, although it was heaven compared to the nights in the Pyrenees. But more about that later.

A cold mist, which made everything moist and clammy, arose from the Meuse. I regularly heard footsteps, at times those of a smuggler and sometimes the regular steps of a patrol on the road. At one time two French policemen with flashlights came by, between us and the river. From time to time, mysterious lights flickered on the rocks. Because you are listening so attentively, you start imagining all kinds of things; in the end you get the idea that "they" are surrounding you and will, screeching war cries, jump on you at any moment and take your scalp. Once or twice I crept back to the hole where Lodewijk and Kloesje lay. Lodewijk had a slight fever, but this fortunately disappeared at daybreak. All in all, it was a memorable night.

The trip to Paris

At first light, we woke up moaning. None of us had slept. We needed to find a place to board a train. This was impossible in Givet because the station was monitored by the police. The next station was in a village 6 kilometres south of Givet. We wanted to catch the train there. By walking briskly, we were just in time to catch the first train. During the 6-kilometre walk, we came across no one. It struck us repeatedly that, in the early hours of the morning, surveillance of the borders was weak; it was, in fact, often wholly absent and we made grateful use of this.

In this town, whose name I have forgotten [Aubrives?], we got tickets to Mézières-Charleville where we wanted to transfer to the fast train to Paris. The train in which we sat was painfully slow and it stopped at every small town along the way. We heard later that it was a train that was regularly checked by the police. This explains the strange way we were being looked at by our fellow passengers; they will have laid bets on when we would finally be arrested.

Kloesje lay sleeping in my arms; she had a serious fever and shivered immensely. We arrived safely in Mézières where we nestled in a café in front of the station. What now? Kloesje's face was flushed with fever and Lodewijk, too, had not quite shaken it. Then we remembered having heard in Holland that in France you could safely turn to the Roman Catholic clergy, because they were completely trustworthy.

We scrounged around for a telephone book and having written down the addresses of several abbots, I left to talk to the men, not only to ask for advice but also for a place to stay until our train left in the afternoon, as we dared not try a hotel without the required papers. I had little luck as none of the priests were home. As I was gloomily walking back to the café, after having climbed up and down an endless number of staircases and having been spoken to and been looked upon with a fair amount of distrust by various housekeepers, I came across a cloister.

Suddenly, the many stories that you read about poor outcasts who get shelter and aid in a monastery sprang to mind. The door to the cloister was open. I walked in and drew the most pious face I could muster. Unfortunately, I did not know that it was a convent and thus forbidden to men. After a while, I encountered a nun who looked at me with horror and who suddenly began saying terrible, angry things to me. I crossed myself to calm her down but that did not help much. How horribly ugly she was! Our Lord can have fun with brides like this. She looked at least a few hundred years old. Before I knew what had happened, I was back in the street and I could suddenly sympathize with our iconoclastic forefathers. Without any result, I returned to the café where I was reprimanded by Kloesje for having stayed away so long. Feeling hurt, I sat down and we said absolutely nothing for a long time.

By noon, Kloesje's fever had just about disappeared. As a result, morale suddenly improved so much that we went for a walk and to look around the town. However, other than the many churches and cloisters, there was not much to be seen and we returned to our starting point soon afterwards. We let Kloesje buy some flowers to hold in her hand. We then took turns walking with her, arms linked, with the other walking a few paces behind and were thus the most innocent looking procession imaginable.

It was finally 3 pm, time to leave. We bought second-class tickets so that we could recuperate from the night before. The train travelled via Reims to Paris, where we arrived in the evening. In Reims, the train stopped for a long while. Train inspection! Kloesje hid behind a German newspaper; Lodewijk and I stood in the hallway casually hanging out to watch all the traffic on the platform. Two soldiers from the *Feldgendarmerie* [German military police] and a man dressed in civilian clothes entered the train carriage and started checking identity cards. Fortunately, there was not enough time to ask everyone to show their papers, so all they did was a spot check; they were kind enough to skip us. It was a very scary moment and we were therefore extremely glad when it was over.

For the rest of the journey, Kloesje occupied herself with speaking very poor German to us, conspicuously reading Nazi newspapers or whispering mysteriously to one of us. Consequently, people in the train mistrusted us immensely and looked at us very maliciously. Kloesje is a master at acting mysteriously, so if you do not know her very well, you would think she was in possession of the most dreadful secrets. During our trip, she succeeded in adorning herself with a mysterious halo everywhere, as a result of which almost anywhere she went people looked askance at her and very evidently mistrusted her. We argued a great deal with her about this, but she could not unlearn it because she would then have had to substitute this behavior with something else, which was impossible because it was simply not there. But more about this later.

In our train compartment sat a Dutchman who began singing the praises of Holland and making it clear that he was not particularly fond of the Germans. He seemed to know Paris very well so I was suddenly interested in him. We had no idea where we should go upon our arrival in Paris. Kloesje's knowledge of the route had been exhausted after we crossed the Dutch border, so we would have to find our own way forward. The man I was talking about could well be an *agent provocateur*. But I did not intuitively think so, and thus I addressed him a few moments later when he stood alone in the corridor. I briefly explained the situation to him and asked him where we might be able to stay the night in Paris. He did not know an address himself but gave me the location of a café in the Latin Quarter where many students always gathered and he advised us to approach one of those people. Again, a remarkable coincidence that precisely that man should come and sit in our compartment!

We arrived in Paris by nightfall. Our first impression was anything but exhilarating. It was raining; no one was on the street and the empty boulevards made a desolate impression on us. We ultimately succeeded in finding the pub we had been referred to, after having asked the way several times and whereby it appeared that it was I who had to speak because Kloesje's "French with a typically Mentone accent" appeared to have abandoned her. She spoke French so badly that mine, which as you know is not particularly great, proved to be brilliant compared to hers. She still just had to get into the swing of things, she said. But I now really wonder when she will finally 'get into it' because these days she speaks most abominably, not to mention how she writes, constantly inserting the phrase: '*Comment s'apelle çà?*', [What do you call that?], into every other sentence.

In the said pub, we did indeed find the students mentioned. The men were of the same satisfied bourgeoisie-type of student as those found in the Netherlands. The women, on the whole, looked well-groomed but rather sensual. One of the girls appeared to be very popular. From this we very astutely concluded that she would thus know many people and so be worth our while as a source of advice about an overnight stay. Kloesje wanted to ask the waiter to request that she come sit at our table and suddenly became very angry when I drew her attention to the fact that one could not ask such a thing of a young lady. I therefore approached the young lady myself and asked her for her cooperation, which she gave readily. One of her paladins was charged with taking us to a small hotel nearby, the Hotel Monaco, in Montmartre where they would also accept us without papers. Half an hour later we lay in bed and fell asleep immediately.

Sens; La Goujauderie

Kloesje had the address of a Dutch farmer near Sens, in the Yonne department. In fact, there is a Dutch farming colony there consisting of some forty families. Most of them have lived there for years.

I had teased Kloesje for weeks in advance about this and had said that we would have to get up very early and milk the cows and such. Then she got very mad and explained that they were not hillbillies; instead they were agricultural engineers from Wageningen [University] who ran model farms there. The idea of resting and having a look around for a while before moving on seemed quite appealing to us, so we cheerfully stepped onto the train to Sens the next morning. Because the train stopped every hundred metres, it was already quite late in the afternoon before we arrived in Sens. Upon inquiry, it appeared that the farm we had been referred to – 'La Goujauderie', the meaning of which no one knew, not even its owner – lay 17 kilometres outside the city and there was no bus or other transport connection to it. Our enthusiasm abated and we went to sit in a café to argue. When that was over, we moved on.

Sens itself is a nice old town with narrow, winding streets and squares with fountains. The road leading to Les Clérimois, the hamlet where the said farm was located, was very primitive and thanks to the rain of the last few days, had turned into a quagmire. Anyway, I best not describe the agony that we had to endure before we stood in front of a large, lonely, castle-like building that turned out to be La Goujauderie. The great gate, through which we entered a large courtyard around which all the buildings were centered, was open. These farms were centuries old and were built in this fashion for security reasons. That courtyard proved to be a horrible quagmire. A tremendous racket made by dogs and geese welcomed us. The people there had already gone to bed as it had already turned 9 pm, which is 11 pm in the country, where people live by solar time.

A dense cloud made everything look terribly sinister and dark. We entered the living room. When we entered the hallway, we started to shout in order to inform the inhabitants of our presence. No answer. Therefore, thinking that there was no one home, we sat down in the 'salon' to await their return. Suddenly a door opened and a man wearing long johns and an undershirt came in. Upon closer inspection, he turned out to be farmer [Huig] Van Kempen. He called his wife [Maartje Buth], who hastily cut some bread and showed us to bed, for which we were very grateful.

The next morning we woke late and in the light we could see the farm better than we had the previous night. I have never seen anything so filthy and unhygienic. Besides the muddy courtyard, the stables, too, were in such a state of pollution that I did not think that a Dutch farmer could ever have borne it. Our host was a farmer from the South Holland Islands, the most unpleasant type of farmer there is, and was reformed into the bargain. His wife was a commoner from The Hague, a sister of a friend of Kloesje's. Here, too, there was a baby in the making and by the looks of it, it would not be long in coming. They were not particularly happy with our presence. Then tactlessly, Kloesje started telling all kinds of stories about nighttime parties at which she was pie-eyed and the like, so that these people held her to be an awful, frivolous creature. The farm staff consisted of a few Dutch who, like us, had fled Holland, a few French and then some Poles. Almost every farm there has a Polish majority.

The food was exquisite; they did not suffer from the war at all. Ham and eggs for breakfast as if it was nothing. We said we were happy to work to compensate for this, but we had arrived at a time when there was little to do, so we usually sat idly.

The people here were terribly pious, always praying and reading the Bible at dinnertime, and howling psalms for hours on Sundays. One time, sitting on the back of his motorbike, I went to church with the farmer; it was a barn painted white and filled with sour-faced fat heads in black, and obese matrons with their offspring. One of the farmers preached. He not only had the largest farm, but also several other farms. Moreover, many of the other farmers were financially bound to him. In short, he was the man with the most influence. It was therefore fair that he should preach.

On the farm there was also a young man of 18, [Jan Hubers], who had come from Holland a year earlier. He had ended up here and having

Jan Hubers at 'La Goujauderie'.

been brought to reason by the good food, had abandoned all plans to go to England and had settled himself on the farm as a shepherd. This young man was happily in the possession of a counterfeit French identity card. When we asked him how he had obtained it, he gave us an address in Sens to which Lodewijk went to enquire. The address appeared to belong to a middle-aged man who had fought in the last war and also in this one; he had a wife, who was a teacher and a daughter, a girl of about 19, who attended the gymnasium.

This man, La Croix, proved to be most charming, particularly when we told him that we were escaped prisoners of war. That was the little white lie that we used when confronted with Frenchmen because it tells them something. Being an exiled student is a phenomenon they do not know and therefore do not care about. This man had a friend who was mayor of a small village called Voisines, just outside of Sens, and he was the one who finally ensured that we got identity cards. Those things were very good: they were real identity cards but were, of course, antedated and they cited birth places that lay in French Flanders, close to the Belgian border which would explain our accents! He also wrote us into the registers of his municipality so that even if further research was done on us, we would actually prove to have come from that town. They were magnificent items. Unfortunately, we destroyed them at the Spanish border, which, looking back, turned out to be completely unnecessary.

When after a couple of days it stopped raining, we had to look after the sheep. That is really an easy task if you have a couple of well-trained dogs at your disposal; but if you do not, then you have to run around the herd continually, yelling loudly and throwing stones. In doing so, you have to make sure that you don't hit them on the head because given that they have a very sensitive skull, they could be dead before you know it. It was an art in itself to keep them out of the clover field, because once they were in that field they ate themselves to death unless you were really forceful with them. And if you thought you had driven them safely past the clover field, suddenly one of those miserable animals would run towards it bleating loudly, as a result of which the entire herd would turn right around and run after that one sheep. All three of us have retained a profound aversion to sheep.

After about a fortnight, the farmer hinted that we should scram. That same evening we got a surprise. Suddenly, outside, we heard someone whistle the Unitas tune, [the first line of the Unitas S.R. corps song] and there at the door stood Armand with two of his friends, Guus Wilderinck and Wim Westbroek, who told us about what had happened in Holland. So rather than just three guests, the farmer suddenly had six, who all had to sleep in the alcove bed for the night. The next morning, the six of us moved on to the next farm near Sens. Here, the farmer and his wife were much nicer, cheerier and more hospitable than those we had met just a little while ago. Farm girl Jo Tromp, a girl of about 22 years old, found the distraction very entertaining. In the evening, a bottle of champagne was fetched and we drank to the success of our trip.

The next day Armand and his friends resumed their journey to the south, although we cautioned them not to leave too hastily. In the end, you are better off considering your options calmly. The principle the three of us adhered to, "slow and sure wins the race", proved to be correct. Kloesje, Lodewijk and I returned to Paris that day to get in touch with the people who, Kloesje claimed, could help us. If we found something, we would let them know. But they didn't want to listen and left. They succeeded in getting a long way, right into the Pyrenees. But there, one of Armand's friends fell to his death. It was Wim Westbroek, a young member of Unitas and a really nice guy. Very tragic. Armand and his other friend were arrested shortly afterwards and taken to a concentration camp in southern France.

Somehow they escaped and finally arrived in Spain. Just before we left for Lisbon, we heard that he was in some kind of prison. Three days after our departure, early in October, they arrived in Madrid. I spoke to him once by phone, but did not see him again after the farm. He is still in Madrid as I write this on 6 December.

Now, our ways split: Armand to the south and we on to Paris.

Paris

Kloesje's "way", which we did not use with the exception of the Belgian border crossing and the farm at Sens (the latter of which was only meant to be a halfway house and did not get us anywhere), now led her to a gentleman who lived in a city about 100 kilometres north of Paris. While she headed towards that, Lodewijk and I travelled to Paris to get into contact with someone whose address we had received from the shepherd. They had been in Switzerland during the war and had taken part in black market trade, as well as other shady business.

This man proved to be a nice guy; very simple. He came from a blue-collar background but was very kind-hearted, with large, innocent blue eyes. His black market trade was very lucrative, but he gave so much of it away to Dutch refugees that he could only lead a humble existence himself.

He could not speak French; his knowledge of Gallicism was limited to two sentences, namely '*Deux demies*!', that is 'Two beers' and '*Oui, mam'zel, c'est la guerre*', ['Yes, mam, that's war']. Armed with this knowledge, he rolled through life, trading on the black market, deplorably cheating the French, flirting successfully with pretty Parisians and ordering food.

His name was Herman Wientjes and he was one half of the company, of which the other half was a previous office clerk with a very keen intellect and an excellent command of languages; he answered to the name of Harry [Bakkes]. We saw relatively little of the latter because he was always terribly busy buying and selling things. Herman, on the other hand, was someone who truly understood the art of living, never took matters too seriously and was satisfied with little. He was a scoundrel, but of the kind with whom, with the best will of the world, you can not get angry and with whom you can moreover have a lot of fun.

Hotel Paris Nord.

This Herman took us to a small hotel near the Gare du Nord train station, where a mysterious Dutch Father [Leo Post] sometimes stayed. He had a parish somewhere in France and hauled young men back and forth. No one has ever known where to or where from, but [the Father] might be able to provide us with information about the south. The hotelier was a suitable fellow, who obviously knew straight away that we were not French, but he pretended to believe it when we assured him that we were.

That night we had just fallen asleep when we were awakened by a terrible racket. Shouting and tramping downstairs, loud banging on the doors and a voice calling 'Police Allemande. Ouvrez la porte!' ['German Police. Open the door!']. The sound came closer. Heavy soldier boots thundered on the stairs as they climbed, excruciatingly slowly, to our floor. Unexpectedly even so, there was a pounding at our door. I'd be lying if I said that we found the situation very pleasant. Well, we opened the door. A soldier from the *Feldgendarmerie* came in and in very poor French asked us for our papers. We did not think that we would need them so soon. We gave him our new identity papers. Having seen Lodewijks's document, the man grunted with dissatisfaction and pointed to the photo; he tried to explain in French that there was no stamp on the photo. The good mayor had forgotten to do this! And when he received my papers, he found the same shortcoming. We now began to find the situation very unpleasant. Gibbering in German, Lodewijk pointed to all kinds of other stamps and tried to get him to see that that there were already so many stamps on the thing that one or two more or less would make no difference. The kraut grunted something, gave it some thought, gave us back our papers and disappeared. We had once more crept through the eye of the needle.

Kloesje, too, had had an exciting night. On her way to her point of contact just above Paris – she insisted on going alone – she discovered that a bomb had fallen on the railroad tracks between the city she was travelling to (unfortunately I can never remember names) and the station just before it. Now you could take a bus, but due to the limited amount of space on these, only if you possessed a certificate from the *Ortskommandantur*, [the commandant of the military occupation authority]. She could therefore not reach her destination and had to stay overnight at the preceding stop because there was no return train. Trains in France run far less frequently than those in Holland do. To make matters worse, all the hotels were full. So, in utter despair, she clamped onto a lady and gentleman in the street and asked them if she might spend the night with them. They agreed immediately and Kloesje went home with them. It was a strange house in which she found herself, with a happy company of beer and cognac-drinking people. After a whole evening of boozing, she was shown a room. But it was an odd room with a curtain instead of a door. Even then, she did not realize that she had ended up in a brothel. That night she promptly received visits from all sorts of guys she thought lived there. She spent the whole night fighting for her chastity and left early the next morning for Paris. Lodewijk and I were greatly impressed by this story; however, now that I know this young woman thoroughly, I take it with a large pinch of salt.

I returned to Sens as quickly as I could in order to get the missing stamp put on my papers. All in all, we were now in Paris with no idea

64

as to how we should proceed. Kloesje had not succeeded in getting a hold of her contact outside Paris and in the city she only had a few rather strange contact points, for example a "guest house" in a certain street. Because she could not specify the guest house further and as the street was crawling with them, it was impossible to find the right one.

Herman kindly helped us. He sent us all kinds of friends who might be able to help us out. For example, he took us to a Dutch millionaire, [Jan Oom], who had left Holland two years earlier with scarcely a thing to his name. By trading on the black market, he had become filthy rich. This man hinted that he did something, work for a secret service or something like that, and that he was willing to help us. He was very friendly, promised Kloesje a new dress and finally came up with a real offer: we could get a job as a worker at the canal defence works. If we discovered anything then we had to let him know. Although we felt highly honoured by this wonderful offer, we turned it down because we wanted to move on.

A young Dutch girl, who had departed just a few days earlier with a convoy of refugees from Holland and had since dropped them off in Switzerland, was among [the friends Herman sent us] and she gave us the address of a Monsieur N., from Lyon, who knew about a certain route. It was the type of route in which you drive in cars to the Pyrenees, then just walk over them and get back in a car awaiting you on the other side.

The millionaire was obviously interested in us, in particular in Kloesje; so he took us to *Monseigneur*, one of the most chic and expensive nightclubs, with an orchestra that continuously plays and is open all night and in which you drink champagne. It became a very strange party. Kloesje flirted a little with the millionaire, which provoked Lodewijk's wrath, which he subsequently cooled with champagne so that he was pie-eyed in no time. I snuck away with the cabaret's Prima Donna; we sat at the bar where I spent the rest of the night with her. She was a girl from North Africa who had been taken to Paris by a guy who subsequently abandoned her. In short, I do not recall the details anymore but it was a real novel. The millionaire busied himself with trying to hear out Kloesje and Lodewijk about their backgrounds in Holland, but they told him nothing. So, we finally had the satisfaction of knowing that that evening had cost him 10,000 francs, approximately 400 guilders, without him getting a grip on us. The Dutch pastor had arrived, but did not know anything either.

Monsieur N. - Peter Naeff

Two days after the *Monseigneur* adventure, Lodewijk and I went to Lyon to have a chat with Monsieur N. In France, too, the trains are packed. If you want a ticket for the main lines, you have to make a reservation days in advance. We hadn't done that and consequently had to stand the whole way, for six hours. It was a nightmare; standing in a crammed train for six hours is no joke. When we passed through the demarcation line, the border between the former unoccupied and occupied part of France, identity papers were checked by the Germans. Aliens are still not allowed to cross that line, even though the French can cross it unhindered if they show their identity papers. Thus we had no problem at all.

We arrived in Lyon at 1 am. Because you were not allowed to be on the streets before 4 am, we hung around the waiting room until we could be on the street. All in all, we were bushed when we finally got a hold of N. at twelve. He worked at a Lyon office of the life insurance company "Utrecht". He was in no way forthcoming, saying that it was completely impossible to cross the Pyrenees and illustrating this with all sorts of frightening examples. In short, it was clear he did not want to help us. So we returned home with no result; after a trip in which we could fortunately sit for half the time, we returned to Paris. (After the war, I heard that he had had contacts that could have taken us further.)

That was not the only trip we undertook from Paris. Regularly, one of us would go to Sens to Jo Tromp's farm, which lies near Sens in a small village called Saligny, to get food. Eating was one of the most difficult problems we encountered in Paris. We had found a restaurant where we could eat well without food stamps, only it was quite expensive, 100 francs or 4 guilders per person. After a few weeks our money supply began to shrink hazardously, so we decided that Kloesje and Lodewijk would go to Saligny and wait at Jo Tromp's farm, until I had somehow succeeded in getting the information and money we needed in Paris.

It was difficult to find the the route, although there were quite a few people who claimed to know something about it. In the end each time nothing materialised. Thus, Kloesje and Lodewijk departed for Saligny and I was left alone in Paris.

Paris (continued)

For me, the next period, which covered more-or-less the month of June, was from a material point of view, one of the most difficult. At the same time, it had also been one of the most educational of the entire trip to date.

The fact that Kloesje and Lodewijk were not present enabled me, to a large extent, to become myself again. I had, of course, gradually come to realize that they were engaged. But if this is the way all engagements go, then I will pass on getting engaged, thank you. Fortunately, there is little likelihood of that at the moment and, thanks to Kloesje, I have had my fill of young girls (somewhat bold imagery here, I daresay!) so this is also unlikely in the near future. With those two it was always stop-and-go; either they were lovemaking non-stop or they were quarrelling with a vengeance. Seeing people necking is something that really irritates me in the long run, so I usually went out for a walk. Noisy quarrelling was also a regular occurrence: Kloesje often did stupid things and Lodewijk, who by the way, I came to appreciate during the trip and who I believe is now a friend for life, was rather short-tempered and expressed his displeasure loudly. Their simultaneous presence got on my nerves during the trip. That's why I was glad they were gone and the certainty that they were safe and well on the farm meant that I did not worry about that either.

However, it was not all fun and games for them there, particularly not for Lodewijk. Every morning at 5 am it was '*Lodewijk, grub up!*' Then Lodewijk had to get up and go to the fields where he had to do hard, heavy work. That wasn't always easy because Kloesje kept him up nights with all sorts of confidential stories. Lodewijk accepted this because he began to understand her better at that time.

Kloesje, too, did well there, doing a little housekeeping, enjoying excellent food, no tobacco and furthermore chatting endlessly with

Jo, the farm girl. Jo was a nice farmer's daughter from Zeeland, still young. However, she had become a little hysterical due to the fact that she was *already* 23 and still had no children. Apparently, that is really awful for a farmer's wife. Knowing that Lodewijk and I had studied medicine she went on and on to us about child bearing and everything connected to this. Poor Lodewijk, in particular, had to hear about her "monthly events" in great detail. But for the rest, they did well in Saligny. It was only Kloesje who, from time to time, was about to go crazy there.

In the meantime, I was almost broke in Paris. Days went by in which I had almost nothing to eat. However, the kind-hearted Herman Wientjes stood by me faithfully. At that time we saw each other almost every day. He was also the one who introduced me to the black market. In the beginning I did not do so well; just about the time I started to get the hang of it, we had to leave. I sold cigarettes, identification cards, cold cream, brilliantine and other toiletries.

In Montmartre, there is a hotel in the Rue Pigalle called Hotel Oria where a lot of Dutch people lived, all of whom were black marketeers. Those guys had left Holland a long time ago and had residence permits. Some of them travelled back and forth to Holland regularly. I asked several of them for favour, which Jos, in the end, gave me.

Many girls from the cabaret, Anime girls, dancers and so forth, also lived in this hotel. I also often saw a Dutch engineer who had lived in Paris for a long time and knew it well. Before the war, he had worked there for an English firm, but after the war he had to work in a French factory for a pittance. That man introduced me to those small, typically Parisian bars. It was not long before I felt completely at home there. You still felt something of the spirit of what Paris was like before the war, a spirit of *joie de vivre* and the feeling of being carefree, despite the difficulties one had in obtaining daily food. It was particularly wonderful in the evening when the girls from the cabaret, the dancers and so on, appeared in these places. They were fun and charming, and when you got to know them better, they were very companionable and did a lot for you.

Parisian women have been criticized – especially in Holland – for their far-reaching immorality. However, in this regard, one must take into account that French morality differs markedly from Dutch morality. Here, one believes that it is natural that if a girl likes a man, she allows him to go far with her. But their rather primitive morality sees no harm in this at all and if you tried to explain it to them, you would quickly discover that they do not understand your arguments at all. By the way, these girls are not the butterfly-like idlers they are so often described to be. As far as I can tell, most of them work very hard as seamstresses, dancers, painters, sculptors and so forth. French women are substantially braver than their male counterparts. They have brains and often great business acumen; many shops are run by women. The heads of some of the largest Parisian department stores and theatres are women. Only, you don't see how hard they work because almost all of them make sure they look very well-groomed. Even this summer, despite the difficulties of war, they really looked good.

The highest fashion was a very large beret-like hat. However, you also saw them wearing flowers in their hair, which looked delightful. I got to know several of those girls very well and appreciated them. We became good friends without sex ever being part of the equation.

A wide variety of nationalities came to these bars, including Turks and Russians. Speaking of Russians, one Sunday, I went to a Russian church service. The congregation consisted of tsarist refugees. Some had worked their way up, but others looked rather poor. Nevertheless, they had fine, civilized faces that immediately betrayed their aristocratic backgrounds. A famous

The highest fashion: a beret-like hat.

Russian church choir, who had made many tours in Europe and America before the war, sang in that church then. I have never heard such a beautiful choir sing live.

The Dutch engineer composed foxtrots and such, and often took me to a studio where he had rented a small room with a piano. A group of ballet dancers also practiced in the same studio. I saw these girls practising and did not envy their work, practising for hours in the morning and afternoon and then performing in the evening. The engineer had a good friend who worked for a Dutch company in Perpignan and he was willing to engage us as labourers so that we could arrive unhindered in Perpignan, calmly have a look around, and then at some convenient moment, walk across the Pyrenees. However, in the end, he was not able to provide us with a position in Perpignan, but instead in Istres, a town just above Marseilles, which was located in a dry and arid region. Because escaping to Spain was impossible from there, this plan was cancelled.

Slowly but surely, I had collected enough addresses near the Pyrenees to venture a trip. Obtaining money was the problem, however. In a weak moment, the millionaire had promised us he would loan us 10,000 francs, but no matter how much I whined, nothing was forthcoming. He was an odd guy, that millionaire. It seems he served the *Schutzstaffel*, [a major paramilitary organization under Adolf Hitler], in the past, but then deserted and went to Paris, where he became incredibly wealthy by doing business with the Germany Army. All in all things weren't going as I would have liked. I could just survive in Paris but that was all, and this way I was not going to earn enough money to successfully push on to the south. Moreover, the information and

Josje - Josephina Wertz

addresses I had collected in Paris were not proving very hopeful. This meant that we started looking at the option of staying in France.

Now, the man from Sens who had supplied us with our personal identification cards was very interested in us. It turned out that he was the leader of a Gaullist group and he offered us work in this line of business. It wasn't very interesting work, but we might well have taken it in the end, if I had not, one fine day, met Jos.

One afternoon my friend Herman and I walked into Hotel Oria, where Herman had to speak to someone. At the desk sat a nice girl who was obviously enjoying good Herman's silly attempts at speaking French. After he had done what he needed to do and we walked away greeting her saying '*Bonjour Mademoiselle*', she, to our surprise, responded in Dutch saying '*goede middag*' [good afternoon], whereupon Herman retraced his footsteps immediately and began engaging the young girl with one of his many nonsense stories. One thing led to another and we went for a drink together. The next evening, Jos and I went out together to a small but exquisite little bar with dimmed lighting and so forth, where I filled her with drinks and subjected her to something resembling a cross-examination. Various people had warned me about her; she was supposedly Gestapo. However, there was no indication of this whatsoever, although Kloesje immediately screamed bloody murder when, a few days later when she happened to be in Paris, I jokingly told her I was dating a Gestapo agent. Indeed, the fact that she had received a return visa for France was a strange thing. She had worked in Paris in the past and, although she had a good job in the Netherlands, she now wanted to look for something in France again. And, in fact, succeeded.

When she heard that we were having financial difficulties, she immediately offered to help us out by getting money for us from Holland as she was going back there for a week to pick up some things. The week before she returned to Holland, we spent time together. It was great fun. We explored the old streets of Paris, ate in small bars in Montmartre, climbed the Sacré-Coeur and did a lot of wonderful things. It was really very nice. Kloesje, however, made me tremble when she phoned from Saligny, with her veiled voice, saying that I must come over immediately. It was for Lodewijk. When I asked her what was wrong with him, she said she couldn't say. I immediately let go of a lot of 10,000 bottles of brilliantine, which I was working on, and ran off to Saligny just to discover that Lodewijk was perfectly fine, but that Kloesje herself was going "crazy". It was a big shock.

Well, Jos left and came back a few days later with your letters which did me a world of good. Oh, yes, the letters caused a bother, too. When she was in Paris a few days before Jos's departure, I told Kloesje that she must make sure that I had their letters – to Lodewijk's and her parents respectively – on time. She promised she would see to it and left again for Saligny. But I heard nothing, so in the end I had to write those letters to Lodewijk and Kloesje's parents myself.

Consequently Jos had quite a few problems with Mamma Parren, particularly because I had mentioned in my letter that Lodewijk was "with his girlfriend" in the country. She was angry with the Parren family. She heard nothing from Mamma Kloesmeijer. Kloesje told me later that she had, on second thought, decided against sending any letters, and had convinced Lodewijk to do the same, because she did not trust Jos.

I was very happy with the good gifts that you gave her for me, particularly for Mother's talisman, which I sincerely believe helped me greatly and I still carry it with me regularly.

The few days after Jos's return, and before she was able to get the money were very eventful.

The talisman De Moulin's mother sent him via Jos: 'Hello my dear boy - take good care of yourself, Mother'.

A couple of days before Jos left, I had met a friend of hers named Evelyn, who also lived in the Hotel Oria. A day or two after Jos's return, I walked into the Hotel Oria, where I needed to speak to Evelyn. There was great consternation among the people I came across there because, early in the morning, the Gestapo had come to arrest all the Dutch. The millionaire, who happened to be there, was also taken. They had just finished telling me the story when the police came back in, two men in civilian clothing, a blond German and a Frenchman. Everyone paled

Evelyn - Jolande Soutif

thinking I would get caught. The extremely kind hotel manager tried to distract their attention by immediately pulling out his hotel book and asking the gentlemen if they might wish to take a seat in the salon and by standing right in front of me so they wouldn't see me.

Evelyn stood by the phone. We already thought they wouldn't see me when the man suddenly spoke to me and asked me who I was. How it was possible, I do not know, but I was able to convince them that I was a Frenchman and Evelyn's lover and that I was there to pick her up for lunch. And somehow or another, they believed me, something which I found totally incomprehensible because these gentlemen are usually not so stupid, and then they walked into the salon. A little while later, Evelyn and I left the hotel, arm-in-arm, chatting cheerfully. This is what one calls "a narrow escape". I didn't feel well for a while either, but providence had evidently watched over me once again. It turned out that there was a raid on the Dutch throughout Paris that day. Immediately, Evelyn very kindly offered me a place to stay with her parents and that afternoon Evelyn and I left by train to Normandy where her parents lived.

At nightfall, after an hours-long train journey, we arrived in the village called Forges-les-Eaux, where her parents lived. Her father turned out to be a railroad worker and illiterate. Her mother was a French farmer's wife and extremely ugly; she had just spent time in jail for distributing pamphlets which had been scattered by English airplanes. There were also about ten children there varying in age from about 20 to about 3 years old. The house was located in the grounds of a chateau and was something of a concierge building next to the farm. But it was filthier than anything I had ever seen. The circumstances in which these people lived and slept were atrocious. Too few beds, so that everything was on top of, and scattered all over, one another.

I was put into bed with daddy. He was a veteran of the previous war with many medals, but I got the impression that he had not had the time or opportunity to wash himself since his return from the trenches. I therefore did not much enjoy that night. The evening was spent in appropriate piousness. Evelyn had brought all kinds of things with her for her brothers and sisters as she had not been home in months and she naturally had much to tell. Everyone was very proud of the beautiful sister who was doing so well in Paris. Evelyn was, indeed, a beautiful girl and brave too. She was not doing at all well when I knew her; she was up to her eyes in debt and had a rather malignant disease too, but no money for a doctor.

The next morning we just messed around in the area. In the afternoon, Evelyn was in pain and went to bed so that I was left to my devices, unprotected with Mamma who did not, of course, view me, the '*monsieur le docteur*', unpleasantly; she amused me with many stories in a dialect of which I understood absolutely nothing. Her youngest little girl suffered from a very filthy rash, which I was expected to look at and diagnose.

Evelyn had to return to Paris and although I was hospitably invited to stay for a few days longer, or even until the end of the war, given the circumstances, I returned with her. We arrived in Paris that evening. At the station there were the usual checks for black marketeers and because I carried a huge suitcase which was almost impossible to lift because of all the butter, cheese, and meat it contained, I felt ill at ease. We had passed by the official safely when, suddenly, from the staircase a figure dressed in civilian clothes loomed saying in a most unfriendly tone: 'Halt! Police!' In my mind's eye, I already imagined us sitting behind bars when it appeared that the man had not directed his attention to me, but to an old woman just behind me whose handbag he went to inspect for dead pigs. Well, 'praise the Lord!'

We were having a nice meal in Evelyn's room when she was called to the telephone. She stayed away for a long time and then let me know that I had to come too. It turned out that Jos was on the phone and not in a very rosy mood. She was unhappy about the fact that

Evelyn and I had left for the country together and when she phoned Evelyn and asked after me, Evelyn calmly responded that I was in her room and could not come to the phone, upon which Jos got very angry and demanded to speak to me immediately. However, Evelyn said that this was not possible, without giving a reason! So while I was upstairs in Evelyn's room peacefully eating a pork chop, the ladies had started arguing about who had the most "right" to me! After we had eaten, I went over to Jos and, after some explanation, set the record straight. Jos was also mad at Kloesje because she had, by chance, been in Paris and after finding me not at home, had looked for Jos's hotel, where she found neither one of us. A little while later, Kloesje had phoned Jos to inform her that she had been to see her in vain and if Jos would be so kind as to come to her straight away, all in a tone that so irritated Jos that it made her say that she would not so much as consider it.

A few days later the money became available at the bank and we could thus leave. It was about time; Paris had started to fascinate me so much that I had difficulty leaving it. Kloesje and Lodewijk could no longer cope with the countryside and moreover a stipulation had been introduced that, in addition to an identity card, one also had to have a "*carte de travail*", a statement authorized by a firm or company that said that the person worked there. Without this permit, your identity card alone was not worth very much.

The journey south

We had decided that Kloesje, armed with the list of addresses we had slowly but surely acquired, would depart alone a few days earlier in order to find out which of the addresses would serve best as a base station for us.

I had great expectations for one address, which I had obtained in rather strange way. One day, as I sat on a bench in Paris thinking about ways in which we might cross to the south, a labourer sat next to me. He had a book by [Swami] Vivekananda on him. I was rather surprised to see a book like that in the hands of a labourer and I asked him about it. It was the start of a really wonderful conversation, from which it appeared that the man was philosophically well-schooled. He obviously noticed that I was not a Frenchman and, assuming that an admirer of Indian philosophers was unlikely to be a collaborator,

I told him that I was Dutch and wanted to go to Spain, upon which he immediately gave me the address of someone in a small town close to the Spanish border, instructing me to say that I came from the "hairdresser".

It is rather dangerous to travel around the south of France because of the many checks on trains and buses, in cafés and on the streets. As women are virtually never checked, Kloesje could safely explore it. We would meet her at a certain time in Toulouse two days later. She departed and two days later, because Lodewijk and I were unable to get seats on the agreed train, we took an earlier night train which departed in the afternoon and which arrived in Toulouse at 11 pm. The hotels were packed so we stayed the night at the station, a rather dangerous activity.

The next day we immediately went to the post office. We had agreed that as soon as she arrived in Toulouse – that is, two days prior to us – Kloesje would leave a *poste restante* for us there as evidence that she had been there and would also, upon returning, let us know in what hotel she was staying. However, there was no letter. So there we stood not knowing whether she had been arrested or not. We were dead tired and went to look for a hotel. Suddenly we saw a well-known figure approaching us: Kloesje! She had written the letters but they had apparently not yet arrived. She had arrived in Toulouse the night before and after having had great difficulty finding a hotel, had been given a room by a hotelier in his own home.

Rooms were to become available in the hotel that afternoon. Until then – it was still very early in the morning – we had to hang around, a very unpleasant activity, particularly if you have not slept the night before, while carrying your heavy raincoats in a sunny, southern climate constantly provoked looks of surprise from those around you. Moreover, in those few days Kloesje had discovered that none of the addresses we had received amounted to anything. So there we were. But we were tired and, more than anything else, we wanted a room. However, the hotelier was very suspicious and so when we finally had the room, we felt pretty uncomfortable. They were, moreover, bad rooms; there was scarcely any water and so on. Now, a poor water supply is common in cities in southern France, particularly in Toulouse where the waterworks are turned off for most of the day. In warm cities, this is very unpleasant. Toulouse, by the way, is known to be a dirty city, even by French standards; here is where "the warm south" actually begins. Lyon is a nice city, built against a steep hill; Toulouse is just dirty.

In the afternoon, we got into an argument with the hotelier, who discovered that what we had written in the hotel register was not wholly correct. As a result, after first having held a long and turbulent war council, in which the same old story, 'Move forward or go back?!' sprang to mind, we decided to try our luck and go to St. Girons, a small town on the border of the 30-kilometre no-go area. Unless you have a reason to be there, you are not allowed in the zone 30 kilometres inland of the French border; checks have been intensified there.

Thus, we departed the next morning more or less with our hearts in our boots. The train took us through a barren, desolate landscape near the concentration camp where we knew Armand was, to Boussens, where we were to transfer to a bus to St. Girons. Having waited several hours in the garden of an idyllic, small café we departed by bus to St. Girons, which lies in the Pyrenees. The road we travelled on was very beautiful; we climbed gradually but quickly and the landscape changed rapidly. It made me think of the landscape in northern Italy where you slowly go into the mountains.

Towards 6 pm we arrived in St. Girons, a nice little medieval town with winding streets and little squares, and divided by a fast-flowing mountain river. A bridge connects the two parts.

Due to some happy circumstance, we did not get out at the end of the line, but at the beginning of the town. At the bus stop there was a check by the French gendarmes, but we managed to avoid this through handy manoeuvering. In a scattered march column we entered the town, in search of a hotel.

To our great disappointment all the hotels appeared to be full, which is a very unpleasant realization in a small town where policeman know everyone and so recognize strangers immediately, and where moreover there are many Gestapo diligently searching for people who want to cross the border.

Finally, we arrived at a hotel at the far southern edge of the city, where we were received with remarkable cordiality and immediately given excellent rooms. After dinner I walked to the office to have a chat with the hotel owner. He came up to me immediately and asked: 'You are a stranger, aren't you?' At that time, I had begun to speak very good French so I was a little surprised to hear this. 'Yes', the man continued, 'just to be on the safe side, I set aside your police papers and have not

Hotel Eychenne in 1966.

Paul Bourdeau, the hotel owner, in 1966.

included them in the hotel register.' He then asked how long we planned to stay, to which I responded that it depended upon whether the area pleased us. He then asked me if we were planning on going to Spain. The man made an agreeable impression on me and because you sometimes simply have to take a risk, I said yes. 'Well you are in luck', he said, 'I am involved in that. Purely for patriotic reasons, so it will not cost you anything. A convoy is leaving on Friday evening, so you can join it.' I was, of course, very happy with this godsend. Just to flatter him a little, I asked him, 'but how do you know we are not with the Gestapo?' This is a psychological question with which you can usually broker success because it indirectly compliments their skills of discernment. In this case, it was a big mistake, but I did not know that then and ran to tell Kloesje and Lodewijk the good news. We spent the evening celebrating with appropriate good cheer.

The next morning when I went to speak to the hotel owner, his response was odd. He said he remembered nothing of what he had said the night before and it was clear that he did not trust us one bit. What had happened?

By chance the day before – the day we had arrived – some thirty Gestapo agents, (including a Dutchman) had arrived in St. Girons to put an end to the many excursions being taken in a southerly direction. This, in combination with my remark about the Gestapo from the night before, had suddenly scared our friend so much that he suddenly remembered nothing. And there we sat. I desperately tried to convince the man of the contrary, but nothing helped. Then I tried to convince his mother-in-law – an ugly old thing of more than 100 years old, I think – by sucking up to her for hours on end and by telling her all sorts of sad stories about us so that in the end, deeply moved, she agreed to cooperate with us.

Her son, (the hotelier's brother-in-law), was summoned. This was a fat son with chubby cheeks; he was from the region and spoke a virtually unintelligible type of French. He promised to look for someone who could help us cross the border. But the trouble was that we had relatively little money left, maybe 5,000 francs. And the gentlemen smugglers requested an average of 4,000 francs per person.

In the afternoon, we had to eat in town because it was the hotel restaurant's mandatory closing day. First Kloesje and I would go and dine; then Lodewijk would go when we got back. Arms linked, Kloesje and I walked into the town. We soon came across a blond man on a bike, who later turned out to be the Dutch Gestapo. After he had passed us, he turned around and, cycling slowly, overtook us, apparently with the intention of hearing what language we spoke. Afterwards, he turned around again and rode away, but when we turned to look shortly afterwards, we saw that he was slowly riding behind us. There was no doubt that we were being followed. This sensation, although thrilling, is definitely not pleasant. This feeling does reach a climax when you arrive at a restaurant and, having sat down at the table, you see the same man enter a little while later and who, after spotting you, steps into a telephone booth. We were convinced that we had been caught and expected to be arrested at any moment. It was idiotic how calm we were at that moment, talking nonsense about how we might best harass the Germans during the interrogation. However, somehow or other nothing happened and we got home unhindered.

In the restaurant we sat next to four French youths in sportswear; it was more than obvious that they wanted to go mountain climbing. One of them even lived in the same hotel as we did. We did not yet know that these four Frenchmen would soon become our travel companions. When we arrived at the hotel, we found out from the hotel owner who the man on the bike had been, and we received the reassuring message that he had moved into the hotel. The hotel hereby suddenly lost its

Left and opposite:
Three of the
four Frenchmen:
Philippe Raichlen,
Hugues Bohn,
Robert Bourcart.
(No photo of Emile
Esande.)

80

charm for us and we decided to leave. But where to? When consulted, the fat brother-in-law advised us to seek accommodation somewhere in the countryside just outside town.

It was now all about leaving the hotel unobtrusively, which was not easy because it was full of Germans who might be suspicious of anyone who left the hotel at night with all their things to go to the countryside. The fat brother-in-law would help us.

The hotel was built around a courtyard. The idea was to cross the courtyard and leave the hotel by way of the side gate. Dimming [the lights] is only superficially practiced in the south of France so it was quite light. Upon his signal, we hurriedly crossed the courtyard, seeking immediate cover behind a car – near the gate we were to go through – when we received a second signal from him indicating "peril". At the gate stood someone who upon closer inspection, turned out to be our friend from the Gestapo. The fat brother-in-law went to chat to him and after a while, he managed to get rid of him, after which we left through the gate and along the backstreets. Soon after, we had reached open country, where we climbed up a ridge from which we had a beautiful view of the lights of St. Girons. But at that moment we were thinking about the awful stories that the old hag had told me about evil Germans with *"grand chiens"*, [big dogs], and we could not find anything funny about the situation.

As we would probably have to wait a few days until the big brother-in-law had something for us, we had to find a place to stay to get us through those days. There were no sheds and so we built a kind of hut in a hedge made of low trees, with leafy branches for a roof, straw on the ground and a low wall of stones around us. We euphemistically called the whole structure our "love nest". Rarely will such unchristian language have been spoken in a love nest as was the case here.

Halfway through the night, it started to pour; a weather phenomenon which our edifice could not withstand. So, after a while, we were totally drenched and cold. The comforting thought that we would not be able to dry and warm ourselves resulted in our uttering many an unkind word. Never had we experienced such a long night. We greeted the following day, which brought us only a very watery sun, with joy.

The food supply was very poor: six pieces of bread each for the entire day. And poor Lodewijk hadn't even eaten the night before. We therefore broke into our emergency rations, a can of condensed milk from Mrs Parren's cellars.

The next day I crawled down the hill and into St. Girons and went to a certain small bar in order to meet with the fat brother-in-law, who would put me into contact with a man who might be able to help us. The brother-in-law was there with a friend and also with one of the four young Frenchmen we had seen in the restaurant. The friend was "*epatant*" [splendid]. He told us that we could most probably leave the next night. Finances and such would not be a problem and would be dealt with later. Extremely pleased, I crawled back to our lair where the mood suddenly changed.

Fortunately, the weather was to remain dry that night.

The next morning I had one last meeting with the fat brother-in-law and his friend. We received some bread and meat from the hotel owner who had, in the meantime, recovered. At 4 pm, the whole party was to meet one another at a certain point along the road just outside of St. Girons. I was to meet Lodewijk and Kloesje a quarter of an hour earlier near the hotel. I waited and waited. Finally they arrived, far too late, as a result of which, when we arrived at the agreed spot, the convoy had already left. I admit that I then lost my self-control and swore profanities as never before. Imagine that, arriving too late for something as important as this.

After we had lost some time by walking back and forth along the river that runs nearby, we decided to try our luck and take the main road to the south. Fortunately, a little while later, we came across the guide who had doubled back on a bike to see where we were. He said that we should stay on the main road until we came across an old man on a bicycle; he would tell us how to proceed.

Indeed, after a while we came across the old man who told us that the road farther down was not safe due to the gendarmes there. Suddenly, a fast-moving car with a loudspeaker roaring something drove up. We thought it was a police car and pretended we were lost. But fortunately it was a car that was loudly announcing the arrival of cyclists in the Tour des Pyrénées, which was taking place that day. After taking cover for a while, we were given a signal that it was safe and that we could move on.

The afternoon was a scorcher and we were dying of thirst. At some point we had to cross a wall which led us to a garden where we found the four Frenchmen who constituted the rest of the convoy. We waited in the high shrubbery until the guide came to get us after the bicycle race had passed the town we had to go through.

We passed through the little town at a brisk march and turned into a wide path that rose upwards rather quickly. The guide, a dark southerner with a goatee, was a young man and was originally a seaman. It was very hot and thirst tortured us. Whenever we came to a stream or a fountain, Lodewijk would drink without restriction which was unwise, given the condition of our stomachs; we had eaten practically nothing since our departure from the hotel a few days ago.

The road was very easy and this in addition to the most charming landscape made the early part of our journey a very pleasant walk. The lower parts of the Pyrenees have the charm of the uncultivated, the areas not yet discovered by tourists, without the grimness of the actual mountain tops. The Basques, the people who live there, are a strange lot, with their own language and strange habits. The villages we passed through consisted of very primitive stone houses. The men all look like murderers and crooks, but as long as you are friendly to them they are kind, decent people. It is a very interesting area with lovely mountain streams and nice, primitive paths. One day, in better circumstances, I would like to spend a vacation here.

In one of the small hamlets, the last one we passed, we stopped for dinner. The French, who were most kind, invited us to eat with them in the hamlet's only tavern. This is when Lodewijk's problems began. He had drunk far too much ice-cold water and had trouble with the last part of our walk. When we were eating, he stood up to go outside but suddenly fell to the floor with a loud thud. We picked him up immediately. His eyes rolled strangely and he was not really conscious. He was very sick. After mopping his wrists and forehead with vinegar, we laid him in bed and continued eating dinner, which was excellent: omelette with mushrooms. Everything tasted wonderful after the forced days of fasting. There was rather a lot of drinking and the company became very merry.

After a couple of hours, the new guide reported for duty. We crossed through the mountains using a well-oiled relay system. We were passed from one guide to the other and everything ran smoothly. The first guide informed us how much all of this would cost. This turned out to be 3,000 francs per person. Among the three of us, we only had 4,000 francs left. So there we were. Again, it was our travel companions who helped us out. We found it very embarrassing, but it was all felt to be self-evident that we accepted it as such.

They were four students who had recently graduated in "colonial administration", what we call internal administration civil servants. Gentlemanly men from very good homes who helped us with everything. Really very nice people, who shared everything they had with us, and as far as provisions were concerned, were well-equipped. Actually, it is thanks to them that, in the end, we arrived in Spain. They were experienced mountaineers who had taken all kinds of tough journeys, such as climbing Mont Blanc, for instance. When at last Kloesje could go no further, they supported and helped her a lot. Unfortunately, I could not assist her; after weeks of very moderate amounts of food in Paris I had enough trouble myself and Lodewijk was more dead than alive.

Initially, the intention had been to cross the border that same night but given Lodewijk's condition, this was not possible. For this reason, the guide took us to a mountain hut – more of a stable really – about an hour or two outside and above the town. We passed right by a German guard post, where the dogs went wild, but where nothing else happened. After a while we waded through ferns as tall as a man and rather damp, and we stumbled frequently. But it was child's play compared to what we had to go endure the next night. Fortunately, we did not know that at the time, otherwise we might have reconsidered. Around midnight, we arrived at the hut where we fell asleep immediately on the dead leaves which lay on the ground.

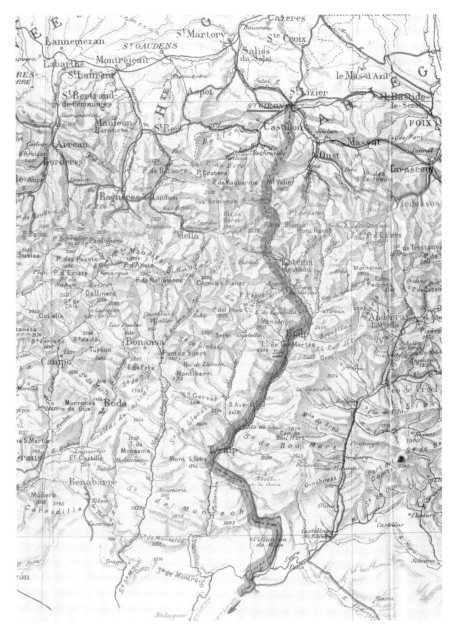

Original map with the route through the Pyrenees as marked by Daniël.

The next morning we woke up late and awaited the arrival of the guide who turned out to be a boy of around 16. We broke up at about 2 pm. Lodewijk had improved greatly and knowing that we would soon be in Spain (the country where – everyone told us with great certainty – we would be lovingly received and be taken care of), for that moment we viewed the future with hope. In a couple of hours, the damned *"Boches"* (these days the French also use the nickname *"les Fritz"*) would not be able to touch us.

That afternoon the trip was very enjoyable. The paths were pleasant and the landscape was very beautiful. It reminded us of the landscape above Montreux, but it was uninhabited. The only life you saw there was a flock of sheep somewhere far away in the valley. By evening we were handed over to a new guide, a shepherd who lived with a colleague in a lonely hut. At that hut, we ate a piece of bread. And then the real journey began.

If at first we had walked on rather easy paths, we now climbed up steep rocks and scrambled over rock piles. For the first time, I had the new shoes on which father had bought for me and given to Jos. In one night those shoes were completely threadbare and destroyed. One shoe broke in two. Kloesje walked on low, laced shoes which she got in La Goujauderie. They were not in such good shape anymore so she was in misery right from the start. Her shoes were broken after a few hours and she then had to continue the trip in a pair of trainers that one of the Frenchmen loaned her.

The trip we made that night was *horrendous*. We slid over glaciers and crawled for hours over rock piles where keeping your balance was very difficult. Sometimes we walked in snow up to our knees. Everything was in pitch darkness. You could literally not see a thing. The guide, who made the trip on clogs, walked ahead of us at great speed and operated Lodewijk's flashlight. Kloesje walked with him and fortunately, he was a great help to her. However, the guide was in a hurry and he rushed us onwards. We got almost no rest. When we had climbed a steep mountain with great difficulty, we saw before us a deep valley on the other side of which was another similarly steep mountain which we would have to cross. It was hopeless. We had to proceed otherwise we probably would not have made it.

We continued to walk, stumbling and falling, tearing open our hands and bruising our knees by falling.

Once, one of the Frenchmen uttered a penetrating scream and then disappeared with a rustle of falling stones into a chasm very close to where we were walking. The scream was blood-curdling and was one of the scariest sounds I have ever heard. We called his name but didn't get an answer. We cautiously bent over the edge and with the flashlight, shined the light into the chasm, the depth of which we could not determine. To our great relief, we saw him lying there a few metres down, fortunately still alive and well. He had fallen on his head and was therefore dazed but for the rest, there was nothing wrong with him. That was a great relief. Imagine if he had broken a leg or something. The misery would have been devastating.

The journey continued, clambering and falling on stones without end, wading through freezing cold streams. From time to time, Lodewijk collapsed. The company then waited a little while, but we had to move on, further and further. Then he picked himself up and stumbled along. It was an unspeakable nightmare. Loesje put on a brave face. Finally, towards dawn, the guide pointed out the final mountain which we would have to climb to get to Spain. The road was a glacier.

We were truly more dead than alive when we finally reached the top of the hill where the Spanish border was. '*L'Espagne, la liberté!*' It was then 9 July 1943.

Spain and our reception there

Weak in the knees, and truly more dead than alive, we descended the mountain to the valley that we saw in the depths below. The first living Spanish beings we saw were a flock of sheep, accompanied by vagrant-like shepherds who, upon our request for shelter, pointed out a hut which lay downstream from the river's origin where we had come across the flock. The landscape was very friendly, but because we were so exhausted, we had little appreciation of it. We finally found the hut where we dropped to the floor as if dead and soon fell asleep.

We woke in the afternoon because the Frenchmen were getting up and preparing to travel. They evidently had not suffered very much from the draft and decided to move on. They wanted to try and catch the train to Barcelona at the closest station nearby. Our physical state was so deplorable that there was but one possibility open to us: go to the nearest *Guardia Civil* post, [the national gendarmerie policing both military and civilian populations], to report and give ourselves up.

There was a farm in the neighborhood that I walked to in the hope I might exchange our pocketknives (which we would have to hand in anyway if we were arrested) for some food. The only living creature on the farm appeared to be a donkey. For the rest, the place was completely deserted. A few hours later, Lodewijk went to have a look and discovered the same thing. So, for a change, we once again had absolutely nothing to eat for the day. We slept in the hut again that night, covering ourselves as best we could with the hay that lay there, but we were freezing.

The next morning, the weather was lovely. The sun shone and the valley looked so friendly. When we left the hut, we met with a Sancho-Panza type of person; a fat man with a donkey that he allowed to graze. In the hope of getting some food from him, we tried to start a conversation. Regrettably, 'Sancho' spoke Andalusian and I spoke 'high Castilian', two languages which differ quite considerably from one another. Moreover, I fear that the Castilian I spoke probably deviated somewhat from what was considered to be general civilized Castilian. Even so, we succeeded in getting a piece of bread and meat from him as well as a sip of wine from his canteen. The Spaniards, who differ from the Europeans in many ways, possess very peculiar canteens; they consist of a leather sack with a cap made of horn with a little hole in it. If you want to drink from the canteen, you have to hold the sack away from your face, then squeeze it so that a small jet comes out of the cap. The challenge is to aim the jet just so that it lands in your mouth, which requires some practice. He told us that a small village lay a short distance away, downstream. Sancho left and we went to the river to freshen up, which was truly needed.

While I was bathing, I suddenly saw Kloesje coming, accompanied by a couple of strange guys in green who, upon closer inspection, turned out to be mountain hunters. After lengthy discussions, it became clear to us that we had to go to the above-mentioned town and report to the police. After informing us of this fact, the guys left us to complete their rounds. That afternoon, we, too, broke up camp.

It was a picturesque procession. We looked like hell: ripped clothing and our complexions varying from sheet-white to ashen. After a march of some hours – which we carried out straddle-legged – we finally arrived in the village late in the afternoon. With some difficulty, we found the guard. With a flourish we gave ourselves up and waited for what was to happen to us. The guard, a corporal, and a bunch of village children didn't really know what to do with us. In the end, we were handed over to a man dressed in civilian clothes who carried an amazingly long rifle over his shoulder at the end of piece of rope. This patriot took us to the gaol consisting of a small wooden building where, to our joy, we were once again reunited with our French friends. In the afternoon, we were interrogated in Spanish by a petty officer, something which led to inquisitive looks from both sides. On the whole, the Spanish, intellectuals included, do not speak other languages. And, many doctors speak very poor French; the majority don't speak it at all.

The terrible thing was that we didn't have any money. The only money we possessed was a few hundred French francs, so Lodewijk sacrificed himself by selling his watch to one of the men guarding us for the sum of thirty pesetas. And if you take into account that a peseta is worth about 15 cents then you can imagine how much he was ripped off.

When it grew dark, we were brought to the lodge under armed escort. Here, we exchanged our francs into pesetas at a terrible exchange rate, but we hoped enough so that we would be able to finance an evening meal. But we had little luck. The neighborhood had so little food that everything had to be supplied to them and the people there were not inclined to let strangers share their dinner with them. So the only thing we could get was some wine, but nothing else. The French provided the landlady with a kilo of sugar and could therefore get an evening meal.

I was able to get the duty officer to allow me, under the supervision of a soldier, to go into town to see what I could get. The only thing I was able to obtain was some goat's milk, which is not very satisfying if you really feel like you will pass out any minute from hunger.

Because we did not feel like sleeping on the ground in the prison that night (where in the meantime, about fourteen Frenchmen had just arrived), we rented a couple of beds in the lodge with permission from the corporal who was guarding us. Kloesje was given the bed belonging to the innkeeper's son, who evidently objected to this, and Lodewijk and I climbed into the innkeeper and his wife's bed.

We had just fallen asleep when we were rudely awakened by a soldier, who informed us that we were expected in the prison. We objected vehemently; we had, after all, paid for the bed and were exhausted. But the local commander, a sergeant, was implacable and so we departed, cursing, for the jail where we were seated on a very uncomfortable, wooden kitchen chair to await the day. By the way, it was very picturesque: a wooden room with a wooden table behind which sat the sergeant. A few Spanish soldiers were hanging around. On the ground lay the refugees. Everything was illuminated by a weak, electric lamp. After an hour, Kloesje arrived, very cheerful, thinking it was almost day and becoming very angry when she heard she had only slept a few hours.

In the middle of the night the sergeant held roll call and after that he gave a long speech of which no one understood a single word. We subsequently had to sign an incomprehensible document. Around daybreak, we broke up.

Lodewijk was ill as a result of the hunger and tried throwing up several times; he did not succeed because there was nothing in his stomach. The road we had to travel to the town where the trucks were to be loaded was a long one. Our suffering had not yet ended. Incidentally, it was a romantic sight; a whole column of refugees – there were about twenty of us – descending along a stony mountain road and supervised by a few soldiers in long overcoats, with caps over their heads and with impressively long guns.

Alos, in the 1960s.

We finally arrived at the town called Alos. You might be able to find it on a good map. We had to wait here for the trucks for a while. With the help of a sympathetic soldier – an exception in Spain incidentally, because the soldiers are generally a bunch of riffraff – we succeeded in buying a piece of bread and cheese which, when added to a cup of coffee with milk, formed a real treat. Lodewijk was too weak to eat.

When the trucks arrived, we were loaded into them and after driving for several hours we arrived in Sort. On the way, soldiers tried to buy everything we had by threatening us with a lack of food. But thinking of the Red Cross and the very active consuls and the paradise awaiting us, we did not succumb.

In Sort, we were taken to a man who proved to be some kind of representative for all consuls; we were interrogated again here. When he asked us if we had any money on us and we answered negatively, we were each given a peseta with which we were to get through the day, because we would not travel further until early the next morning. In Sort itself we had freedom of movement. Those with money could stay in a hotel; those that did not had to stay in prison for the night. That day we strolled through town and 'squandered' *all* of our money on buying bread and sardines, and coffee with milk. 'Café con leche' is truly delicious everywhere in Spain and over time we drank litres of it. Kloesje was accommodated in a strange sort of guesthouse by our host and Lodewijk and I reported to the prison where we were received and locked up by our host, who also turned out to be its warden. It was a medieval dungeon with huge bars.

Besides us, the den was also inhabited by a very awful looking gentleman who had also come from France, where as communist, he had fled after the Spanish Civil War. However, driven by love, he had now returned and had had the misfortune of meeting up with a policeman who knew him personally and who had promptly arrested him. Hoping that our inmate would not murder us during the night, we climbed up the iron frames that were supposed to be beds and fell asleep.

At dawn we were woken by the *Guardia Civil*, one of those fellows with a strange triangular hat on like you see in the photos, and we were loaded onto a bus to Lérida where we arrived several hours later.

Paradise

Lérida is a town which played an important role in the Spanish Civil War. It was besieged for a long time by the Germans and Italians and traces of this can still be seen clearly in the form of houses which have disappeared, holes everywhere from rifle and machine gun fire, and damaged bridges. Lérida is primarily a left-wing town and the fact that its reconstruction is taking so long is not only due to general Spanish laxity, but must also be largely attributed to harassment by the government.

Under armed escort, we were brought to a government building where Kloesje was taken inside and the rest of the group had to stand in front and wait for hours in the burning sun. Kloesje did not return and we were taken to a grim and very unfriendly looking building that turned out to be a prison. Here everything we possessed, such as pocket knives, razors and scissors, was taken from us. We were subsequently taken to a barber who, with great virtuosity, totally and radically removed all our hair so that we came out as bald as billiard balls. This and other things made us start to believe that the situation was a little suspicious and after we had spoken to the internees who had been there longer, it appeared that this was to be our "home" for the coming months, our enthusiasm began to drop drastically.

Soon afterwards, it was dinnertime. A trumpet was blown and from all sides internees walked up, all with bald heads, and began lining up in two columns, each of which was about ten men wide and twenty to thirty men long. The columns slowly slid towards the area where the meal was being served into the tin bowls everyone held in their hands. It was exactly like you see in the movies. The meal consisted of a watery rice soup with a little layer of olive oil on top and a small piece of bread. Everyone tried to eat the soup as quickly as possible and then went back to stand in line in the hope of qualifying for a second portion.

After dinner, Lodewijk and I sat in the courtyard bathing in the sun. Suddenly a very strange person, who spoke an even stranger language, stood in front of us; upon further scrutiny, he appeared to be from the Dutch province of Limburg. This illustrious character was the only fellow country man there and his name was Peter Veuglers. For the most part, the refugee-prisoners consisted of Frenchmen, usually scum from Ariège who hiked over the Pyrenees when things got too miserable in France.

Most of them had hangdog faces, which were accentuated all the more by their shorn heads. "Our" Frenchmen were just about the only polite ones in the company, which also consisted of some Poles and a couple of Belgians.

The prison had once been a seminary, which was obvious from its construction and from the name 'Seminario Viejo', which means 'old seminary'. Along with the centuries-old citadel, it lies on the top of a hill up against which the older part of Lérida was built. It was originally a prison for political prisoners, who were apprehended

92

Lérida (now Lleida) Prison, 1966.

during and after the civil war, and who still form a large part of the Spanish population. The buildings lay on three sides of a courtyard. Two wings were still inhabited by political prisoners, the third was for refugees. Sentries stood with loaded guns on the rooftops making escape impossible; just before we arrived someone was shot by one of these scoundrels just because, according to the sentry, he stood a little too far in front of (of all things) a *barred* window!

Full of enthusiasm, Veuglers dragged us to his quarters; a room about 30 metres long and 10 metres wide. Some 200 men were housed here. Some of the more fortunate who had been here longer had a straw bag and a blanket; pending this luxury, you had to lie down on the red stone floor for the first few weeks. Besides the prisoners, this attractive residence was also inhabited by bedbugs in huge numbers, as a result of which the majority of the men were covered with red spots and a rash. Most of them scratched themselves until they bled, after which the wound began to fester. There was only one toilet for the entire room and it was incredibly filthy; the smell ruined the entire atmosphere and there was one tap which only worked in the evenings and at night. All of this gives a faint impression of the desperately wretched conditions in the Spanish prisons. Bullet holes at a man's height in the walls were witness to the work that the firing squads had recently done there.

During the afternoon visiting hours, Kloesje came to see us, accompanied by a representative from the Dutch consulate in Lérida. This man, Jaus, who only spoke Spanish, had been appointed to this venerable post because he happened to work for the Philips factories. But that is all that could be said of him. We spoke with him in a room that had been divided by two grids which stood about a metre or so from one another. Kloesje and the representative were on one side of the barrier and we were on the other. Because we were not the only ones who had visitors, everyone tried to speaker a little louder, and consequently the shouting and ranting could be heard from afar.

From what we understood of Kloesje's shouting, she was in the government building (into which she disappeared while we had to remain standing in front of it) where she had come into contact with the secretary of the Lérida province, an influential man who claimed that he liked the Dutch. This liege had put her into a hotel and had promised to get us out of prison, primarily because we said we were doctors, as this is what Lodewijk had kept saying about us while we were in Spain. There was little danger in doing so because someone with a Dutch bachelor's degree in medicine knows ten times as much as the average Spanish doctor. It also has other advantages because, according to the Geneva Convention, you are more or less untouchable. Kloesje advised us to go to the warden and vigorously insist on better accommodation. She also promised to send us food from the hotel on a daily basis. She departed promising that we would get out soon.

Soon afterwards we met the warden, a proud, conceited, dumb and cruel gentleman, decorated with the necessary medals (every self-respecting warrior or policeman in Spain pins some medals onto himself – the more the better) and to whom we protested loudly. This, in combination with a personal phone call from the secretary, resulted in him conceding and, as a favour, sending us to the sick bay – as if we were sick – to be accommodated more favourably. This is a typically Spanish form of honour: large numbers of prisoners are laid in the sick bay, even if this means that the genuinely sick (there are enough) have to be removed from it.

We spent five days in this sick bay, right up until we were released from prison. These five days were very interesting and educational, in part because political prisoners were also housed there. Each of us was designated – oh what a luxury – a sort of bed. A man had recently died in mine and Lodewijk's sheet also looked yellow. But this fact was apparently no motive for the prison management to wash the bed linen. So, we closed our eyes and crawled into bed. The dirtiness of the sheets was not the worst thing; at night whole regiments of lice arrived to make your life miserable, particularly because we had been so unwise as to turn and shake our mattresses. We were enlightened because of this and in the morning we restricted ourselves to only carefully closing the bed linen after which things improved. Compared to the situation in the cells, this was paradise. The room was under the command of a doctor and a couple of orderlies, who themselves were interned political prisoners and had not left the room for five years.

The doctor, an elderly republican, was not very militarized and had entered into a state of far-reaching apathy This meant that the surgery hours were held by the orderlies, who energetically used the same pair of tweezers they had just used to pull out a toenail as they did to pick at the next patient's molars. The medicine this miracle worker had at his disposal – aside from bismuth for dysentery, from which a large portion of the Spanish prisoners suffered, sometimes in terrible epidemics – was a pink and a white cream, the consistency of which remained a mystery to everyone; both were kept in empty jam jars. Incidentally, the orderly was a friendly fellow and thanks to him we didn't have such a bad time there.

A pair of French doctors also lay in the room. Opposite them it was difficult to sustain that we, too, were doctors, but we did succeed. One of them was a marquis, who concealed his aristocratic name under the pseudonym Doctor Violet. The other doctor also used an alias and called himself Jean Latour. After a while we discovered that he was not a Frenchman but a Russian. The latter lay in the bed next to Lodewijk and turned out to be extremely nice. He was incredibly ugly and his appearance was not much improved by his wearing a leather vest with corduroy trousers, the crotch of which hung between his knees. He shared everything he had and was also a good pal in other ways. We became good friends with this man; quite long after we left the prison, we still wrote to each other. The marquis was a nasty fellow, artificially funny and extremely stingy so that we had little contact with him.

One of the other guests was a rich Spaniard who received a large basket of groceries and clean bed linen every day. First he didn't grant us so much as a glance, but when we, too, received a large basket of food, we rose in his esteem. There was furthermore an old Spaniard there whom we hardly noticed at first because he was so quiet and self-absorbed. That was understandable: the war council was deliberating whether, after five years in prison, they should still execute him. Two days later, his death sentence indeed arrived. He kept a stiff upper lip.

He was a very gentle man of advanced age, but prison had made him look far older than he really was. We spent his last night together. The conversation drifted to Andalusian folk dancing and songs. One of the orderlies demonstrated the dancing and the condemned man sang in accompaniment and stamped his feet. It was a tragic thing to see. Early the next morning, he was taken away.

And thus a staggering number of people still die in Spain even now as I write this, in January 1944. Franco is a very blood-thirsty person with very limited skills. Leaving state matters to his ministers, he is primarily interested in eating, movies and bull fighting. It is said that he is a homosexual. His government will probably only be of short duration and will not survive the end of the war for long. While we were there, the "man in the street" already spoke openly about the coming revolution. The latter is very likely to take place because starting a revolution is something the Spaniards enjoy doing. Hopefully, in the next revolution those who have nothing to do with it will not get involved, like the Germans and Italians did in the last civil war. Spaniards fight in a gentlemanly way: they begin after breakfast; during the hottest part of the day they rest a while and around nightfall both parties go home and neither can be induced to continue fighting through the night. The indignation among both parties was great in the last war when the Germans continued to fight through the night and even attacked during this time! In the end, you have to respect the rules of the game.

On the second day of our internment, Kloesje came by again to honour us with a visit. This time, she was neatly decked out in a grey suit and, thanks to an artificial intervention by a hairdresser, her hair was considerably lighter. Slowly the days crawled by and finally on the sixth day, we were taken out and brought to a small hotel, [Hotel Pepe], into which Kloesje had moved.

Kloesje was there in the company of the secretary of the province, a young man who stemmed from one of the foremost families in Madrid and who answered to the name of Poveda. We apparently arrived at an

De Moulin and Parren after their release from the prison in Lérida.

inopportune moment because the young lady responded icily towards us. The next morning we were dragged around town by the Philips man, who bought all sorts of essentials: shoes, toiletries, underwear and a new pair of trousers for me.

Almost immediately after our release, the conflict between Kloesje and Lodewijk resumed and it persisted *sempre crescendo* until Lodewijk and I left Spain; it completely spoiled our lives during this time and drained all our spirit and energy. In short, Kloesje had broken off with Lodewijk. This simple fact could have remained just that if both parties had not blown it up into something so large that I, too, could not stay out of it either, particularly when this and that resulted in my losing all control over Kloesje; without being able to do anything about it, I saw how she plummeted and began to lead a very dubious lifestyle.

In addition to the many quarrels between her and Lodewijk – in which she said very unkind things to him which hurt him deeply because he still loved her – she did everything she could to bring us down as much as possible. To start with, she clearly demonstrated her contempt for us in front of the hotel staff, and because they all adored her, particularly the management, this resulted in our being treated badly and rudely. Moreover, she regularly went out with "very important" people. Just what happened in Lérida, I don't know but

Robert Bourcart: Villa Lac Providence
Route de Vaux. Royan'–

Emile Escande
53 rue des Bezines
Angoulême

Philippe Rouicklen –

Hugues Bohn

André Musset: 12 Av= Kalvesin
of DEF. 18-72   courbevoie

v=lle Roel Kloesmeyer . C/o P. Stauberger
54 Kaserne Straat – Den Haag

Louis Pazzen – Zalsbommel –

Damiel de Moulin. v=t Melstlaan 19
Naarnen

– Jean L'Herbette   10 rue de St Etienne
Rabbat

– Raoul Delaye   7 Av= de Ble Knes
Rochbat

Address list of Hugues Bohn with the names of the French and Dutchmen.

98

from the fact that the Dutch consul in Barcelona felt compelled to write a report about her to the consul general, it is obvious that it was not "normal". Theoretically I was the same person for her, but the fact is that I was not because she kept me out of everything.

It was from that point on that her *Geltungsbedürfnis*, [her craving for recognition and prestige], began to take on forms that were frighteningly abnormal. She was going to reform Spain, offered us good jobs, and only went out with "important" people. She started looking bad as a result of alcohol and staying out late partying. I unceasingly tried to play the intermediary and to absorb the blows from, and for, both sides. This situation, coupled with the awful material conditions in which we found ourselves – the hotel was very poor, the food was sub-standard, we had virtually no money – ensured that were very happy when, after a few weeks, secretary Poveda allowed us to depart for Madrid. Before then, Kloesje was successful in getting the four Frenchmen with whom we had come, as well as our friend Veuglers, out of prison.

One of the Frenchman was a little in love with her and as a souvenir, he gave her a small diamond ring which his grandfather had given his grandmother when they had become engaged. Later on, she sold the ring in Madrid in order to obtain the money she needed for her crazy lifestyle. I wasn't supposed to know about this, but I found out anyway and I resented her for it, given the gesture and the feelings with which the Frenchman had given her that ring.

Madrid

After a long and incredibly filthy journey by train, we arrived in Madrid on an evening in early August and settled into the hotel we had been assigned. This hotel, with decent rooms and staff dressed in black, seemed like paradise after the beastly hotel in Lérida and the deprivations we experienced prior to this. One drawback to this hotel was that it was located on a busy street along which ran many squeaking trams.

The following morning we reported to the consulate, an activity we would repeat many times thereafter. From the consulate we received vouchers with which we could go to the various shops and buy essentials, a nice suit, shoes, and so forth. Upon arrival, we also received 100 pesetas and thereafter 60 pesetas per week in pocket money and a voucher every day which we could use in a lunchroom for a free cup of coffee, tea or ice cream. The food in the hotel was reasonable. I can add nothing further to this other than that, from a material point of view, we were very well looked after.

Moreover, the Dutch had the privilege of being allowed to make use of the fascist party's pool, a really nice place where Lodewijk and I could be found almost every afternoon. Incidentally, there was nothing else to do. Lodewijk started buying large amounts of oranges and promptly got sick.

Madrid itself isn't a bad city. With the exception of the city centre, it is young and therefore has relatively modern buildings. However, as is the case elsewhere in Spain, it is not "finished" anywhere. The inherently beautiful boulevards leave an unfinished impression because, for example, the pavements have not been tiled, consisting instead of stamped down earth between stone curbs, which form glorious mud pools when it rains. There are many monumental buildings, some very beautiful, but they are largely imitations of foreign building styles. With the exception here and there in the city centre, you see relatively little Spanish architecture. The post office, for example, is a huge building which exhibits every conceivable architectural style from ancient to modern times. Really very beautiful are the large wrought iron doors in the big buildings, which themselves are often very artistic.

Although various parts of Madrid, including the 'cité universitaire' [university centre] were completely destroyed during the civil war, on the whole, it survived the civil war graciously. It is thought that Franco wished to spare the city; there may be confirmation for this in the long duration of the siege.

It was extremely hot at this time of year. However, I was content; the climate made me think of that of Batavia, a dry heat during the day and in the evenings, a delicious, sultry temperature.

Kloesje instantly started acting as if she was very important, consequently alienating everyone as a result of which we, her travel companions, were also regarded with a wary eye. Now, it didn't bother us so much because the level of the Dutch refugees in Madrid was depressing. A very large percentage were Jews and the rest were all sorts of adventurers and just a few "decent" people.

Kloesje directly started making sharp, anti-Semitic remarks, which was not very wise. Thanks the fact that one of those working temporarily at the consulate was an acquaintance of hers, she got to

De Moulin's identification papers from the Spanish and Portuguese authorities.

know a couple of nice people, whom she kept far removed from us. One of the Dutch women whom she got to know via one of these people, was going to give her Spanish lessons, but nothing came to fruition, despite her huffy, full of wind attitude and instant criticism of my Spanish. This is because she is incapable of seeing through anything which requires any kind of intellectual effort and after a few lessons, she quit. She did not want to introduce us supposedly because the lady was too civilized for Lodewijk! Her selfish and self-centred character is clearly demonstrated here: her acquaintances were hers and she did not want to share them with us. She was extremely demanding at the hotel, never came to the table on time, and created scenes in which she got up and left.

You may be asking yourselves why we still "put up" with this. Looking back, I am not sure either, but it was because I felt responsible for her, because she was so young, because officially we were still good friends and because I thereby still had some, if very limited, influence on her; an influence I tried to use for good. It saddened me greatly to see this girl, whom I had loved very much, not as a member of the opposite sex but as a good friend, go to hell, and it was for this reason that I accepted many unpleasant actions and even insults.

She hung around with many questionable characters in bars for nights on end and was consequently insufferable the next morning. I knew some of those characters, all of whom were typified by her as "very important", including a few Belgians. Now, I have never been able to put up with Belgians very well, but since then I would gladly see them all drop dead and if I now come across a Belgian, I instantly start talking with him about their king and the Ten Days' Campaign, [a failed military expedition by the United Kingdom of the Netherlands against the secessionist Kingdom of Belgium in 1831]. According to her, one of these Belgians was one of the most promising pilots in Belgium, someone who had fought fiercely in the war and who was very important to the Allies. He claimed to be a count, which immediately impressed Kloesje, and she informed us that he would ask her to marry him and that she would say yes. However, he was too wise to ask that pernicious question. I did not take the miserable and insignificant little man very seriously and I upset Kloesje once when the little count politely greeted me saying 'Good morning, doctor' (Kloesje always tells her friends that Lodewijk and I are doctors, just to seem more important) and with my index finger I poked him in his belly and said 'Hey, count!' I met the little man again later in London. He turned out to be neither a count nor a great pilot.

Now this little count was a pretty innocent person, but there were quite a few darker and more dangerous characters around who originated from the political underworld all over Europe. The crisis was inevitable and it finally came.

Hendrik emerges, as well as other characters

In the preceding chapter I mentioned something about some people Kloesje got to know at the consulate and whom she carefully kept removed from us. One of them appeared to have a special interest in her: he went out with her a lot, and visited her room frequently. Looking back, it was quite understandable because he had just gotten out of the infamous concentration camp at Miranda, and she was the first Dutch girl he had met.

Lodewijk and I had been allowed to go along a couple of times when they went out and those times we liked the young lad a lot. He came from a good family and answered to the name Jan Willem Gaillard Jr. However, he had lived in the concentration camp as an Englishman in the hope of getting out sooner and he had given himself the name Henry Lons. But as neither Lodewijk nor I are Anglophiles, we rechristened him Hendrik, and nicknamed him Hendrikje, which he first greatly objected to but later accepted so that he now comes running if you call him by that name. He also turned out to be a student from Utrecht and had almost completed his studies in Dutch East Indies law. You can see an example of his face in the photo below of two petty officers of the Royal Netherlands East Indies Army.

Now, Lodewijk and I thought this young man was too nice to allow him to get caught up in Kloesje's nets, so we decided to visit him one afternoon and warn him. One thing led to another and in the end we became fast friends, especially from the moment we all started living together. At a certain point, Lodewijk and I felt obliged to leave Kloesje alone and move. A big scene was the occasion for this.

One evening Kloesje was very sick. She had a fever and was delirious. It was late but kind Lodewijk hurried away and managed to

Daniël de Moulin and Hendrik (Jan Willem Gaillard Jr.) as petty officers in the Royal Netherlands East Indies Army (KNIL).

get some ice. Because we did not trust the situation, we decided to take turns keeping watch on her that night. Lodewijk was to be on watch the first night. I had scarcely fallen asleep when suddenly someone wrapped in a sheet stormed into my room, followed by a horrified Lodewijk. She had woken up, had seen Lodewijk and had ordered him to leave, which he had refused. After fighting, she came to me and said all sorts of coarse things. That closed the door on our relationship and I then told her to leave my room.

The next day she apologized and because we blamed her behaviour of the previous evening on her feverish condition, we decided to try it again one more time. But it did not work. We tried to exercise the utmost patience but it was unbearable, so we decided to move. This decision is one of the most difficult ones I have ever made in my life, because I realized that she would go to the dogs more quickly then. But the fact that she would also go this route with us there, and that the only result would be that we would go *with* her, prompted us to take this decision. We really had been so ill-treated mentally that we experienced the consequences for months afterwards. One evening we shared this with her resulting in yet another dramatic scene, which I best not describe here.

Shortly afterwards, we left the hotel and settled in the Asturias Hotel, one of the best hotels in Madrid and in which only under exceptional circumstances the Dutch were placed by the consulate. Because we were on such good terms with one of the envoys, who had read our report [on the Dutch student resistance] and was very pleased with it and asked us to dinner and so forth, we were held in rather high regard.

A few days later, Hendrik also moved into this hotel. We stayed there for about a month and had a wonderful time. The hotel staff did not understand us at all. In the dining room and so on, we behaved very well and walked around with the haughty faces which such situations require. But on the other hand, we took pleasure in things that were incomprehensible to a Spaniard. We stacked furniture up against the inside of each other's doors so that when you got home a whole pile of things fell on your head with indescribable noise; we tipped each other's beds on edge so that when you went to sit on it, it collapsed; we had water fights and all of this preferably in the middle of the night. Hendrik was the primary victim of all of these jokes. But because he has a good sense of humor, which is one of the main reasons we like him so much, he always enjoyed it too. It was a wonderful time and a real relief after the previous period.

Harer Majesteit's Gezant

heeft de eer ter Uwer kennis te brengen dat hy op 31 Augustus a. s. tusschen 11 en 12 uur v. m. op Harer Majesteit's Gezantschap, 6, Casado del Alisal, de gelukwenschen die Nederlanders aan H. M. de Koningin zouden willen uitbrengen, in ontvangst zal nemen.

Madrid, 20 Augustus, 1943.

Queen's day 1943. Invitation for the reception at the Dutch embassy in Madrid.

Her Majesty's envoy is honoured to inform you that, for those wishing to express their best wishes to Her Majesty the Queen, he will receive these at Her Majesty's Mission, Casado del Alisal 6, on the morning of 31 August from 11 am until 12 pm.

We came into contact with the woman who Kloesje was to take Spanish lessons from. She had lived in Spain a long time but was a bit of an outsider to the Dutch colony. Mrs Ligthart was a very sweet women of about 60 years old, although you wouldn't give her more than 50. She loved merriment and we visited her frequently. She always made sure that there was wine and she threw parties for us several times, even though she really didn't have much money. She was always called Sophie. She truly did give us a lot of joy and we think back on her with immense gratitude. It was a very pleasant month in which only our chronic lack of money and Hendrik's girlfriends were our only worry.

In the meantime, Kloesje went out with a certain [Felix Theodoor] Schölvinck, a man who had been sent from Lisbon to Madrid to sort out money matters. Indeed, the consulate really was a mess; even after three years of war, refugee care had still not been organized. In Madrid, we got a little foretaste of the hopeless, sad and irresponsible mess found in London. Kloesje moved in with this man after our departure and it is said that she became his mistress.

105

About ten days before our departure another lady came to live in our hotel: Mrs Rutten, the wife of the one who, back then, had made the film *Dood water* [Dead Water]. Shortly before that, she had left Holland. She was a really nice woman and pretty tightly wound. Her name was Ems, but because we thought that was too long, we called her Cecile. We had a lot of fun with her, too. But it was only for a short time because our Portuguese visas were ready and so our departure date drew near.

On 29 September, we were taken to the night train to Lisbon by a whole procession of people. All kinds of girlfriends of various nationalities came around to see us off. At the last minute, Sophie – very kindly – gave us a bottle of cognac for the journey. Kloesje was there too, accompanied by Schölvinck. She looked pale and smelled of alcohol. Of course, a great kissing fest took place in which we kissed all of the women present. It was a strange farewell.

There is nothing worth mentioning to tell about the trip to Lisbon; it lasted the whole night which we, with the help of the available spirits, spent in "suitable" joy. The three of us shared a first-class coupé and we all found it a strange experience to cross the border normally.

Portugal

There is actually little to tell about the month we spent in Portugal. Our primary activities consisted of eating, drinking, sleeping, swimming, walking, playing poker and being bored. Because the Portuguese police don't want to have any refugees in Lisbon, the Dutch refugees are concentrated 20 kilometres north of Lisbon, in a small bathing resort called Praia das Maçãs.

It is a small resort by the sea. The coast is very rocky and steep, with relatively short stretches of beach here and there where you can swim. The climate is delicious. The tourist season had just ended when we arrived so it was rather quiet there. Because the two guesthouses requisitioned by the Dutch were packed, we were accommodated in a house in which the only furniture was beds. We ate in the guesthouse. Thus, the housing was rather primitive.

It wasn't very pleasant, at least that is what I thought, despite the beautiful landscape. We were there with a large colony of Dutch, again primarily Jewish, in a tiny village. You couldn't walk anywhere without coming across them. There was also a Jew in our room, as we had a four-person room, but he was a very nice fellow. This character soon became the target of our jokes. Then he began to moan saying that we held "one-man pogroms". Every evening there was a lot of noise in the room, great "fights" that lasted until the furniture collapsed into a thousand pieces on the ground. That sounds worse than it was. The beds consisted of iron skeletons upon which iron rods rested, which in turn supported the planks upon which the mattress lay. Hence East Indies beds. If you knocked a bed like that over, then a deafening noise arose because everything fell apart and fell to the wooden floor. Hendrikje's bed, especially, was a favorite target and so every evening, without fail, it was toppled. This was because the bed was turned lengthwise towards the wall against which the headboard stood, so that the buck-naked and screeching Hendrikje – boy, did he yell! – stood on his head wedged between the wall and the bed and buried under the mattress and planks. That was a sight which never bored us and gave us satisfaction every evening anew. Large crowds of villagers often stood listening in astonishment to the indescribable noise. More than once we were called to order by the colony's leader.

We received 100 escudos per week in pocket money, which is about 8 guilders. However, Portugal is an expensive country so you really do need it. From time to time, we went to Lisbon. Lisbon is a relatively small city, but it isn't bad. The centre of town consists of a wide boulevard called the Avenida da Liberdade. This boulevard, planted with palm trees, is very modern and it is a great place to sit. Portuguese architecture, both the old and the new, is extraordinarily nice and has something really special about it. The lower edges of the roofs bend upwards slightly, just like Chinese roofs do. The walls of the houses are often partially or completely covered with tiled ornamentation, proverbs, saints, images above the door and such. The tile industry owes its existence to the fact that old trade ships transporting tea from China used tiles as ballast for the ship.

Management of the Dutch embassy here in Lisbon is far better than that in Madrid. While in Madrid the chancellery and consulate were housed in a couple of rooms somewhere above a courtyard in a small residential area. Here in Lisbon, it consisted of a proper building with many large rooms and located in a good neighborhood opposite the Technical College. There is even a sentry box in front of the building; it looks almost real. At the time, it was put there by the Portuguese to

Hendrikje, Daniël and Lodewijk at Praia da Maçãs, 1943.

house a soldier with a real gun, who was there to protect the legation from potentially angry mobs at the time when the Dutch occupied Portuguese-Timor during the war with Japan. The Portuguese have taken this fact into account calmly. Incidentally, the legation personnel were jealous of the English, who got an entire machine gun nest in front of their legation. People work hard at the legation and the atmosphere is better than in Madrid. The staff is extensive, there is a good secret service, and so forth.

Since Portugal is the only neutral country in Southern Europe, Lisbon is a pleasure ground for espionage and counter-espionage. You cannot really call Spain neutral; even now, on 27 January 1944, it is still sympathetic to Germany, although not as much so as it was two years ago, for example. The fact that Franco dissolved the Falangist movement, similar to the SA and WA, [the paramilitary arm of the Nazi Party in Germany and the National Socialist Movement in the Netherlands, respectively], incidentally proves that Spain is coming around.

A few days after our arrival we were checked for the military service. This was done by Portuguese doctors, who are far better than the Spanish, who speak excellent French and English. The results were sent to England, where the Dutch Inspection Board determined whether you were approved or not. Being approved is a *conditio sine qua non* to get into England; if you are rejected, then you have to wait *ad infinitum* for people in England to summon you, which sometimes takes months.

Our surprise and disappointment were great when the results showed that Lodewijk had been rejected and Hendrik and I had been approved, in the highest class even! One is no longer rejected on the basis of your eyesight, unless you are blind. It was crazy. Lodewijk, who had already been in the service, was now rejected and I, who had been rejected twice already, was now approved. That meant that we had to part, something we both found very distressing.

On the whole, those who went to England were transported to Gibraltar by boat and then from there by boat again to England. That takes a couple of weeks. Neither Hendrik nor I felt like doing it this way and we got someone to send us by airplane.

And so, on the evening of 27 October, Hendrik and I were taken to the airport by Lodewijk and a man from the legation. The farewell

L E V E N S B E S C H R I J V I N G.

Daniel de Moulin,

geboren te Buitenzorg op 12 September 1919.

Schoolopleiding. Lagere school te Buitenzorg. Daarna bracht ik eenige jaren in Europa door en bezocht het Lyceum te 's-Gravenhage. In 1934 ging ik terug naar Java (Batavia), waar ik in 1939 het eindexamen gymnasium B aan het Bataviaa sch Lyceum behaalde. Eind 1939 ging ik naar Nederland terug, om aan de R.Universiteit te Utrecht medicijnen te studeeren. Van het begin af aan heb ik intensief aan het studenten- leven deelgenomen, wat tenslotte culmineerde in het bekleeden van een der meest vooraanstaande plaatsen in het verzet tegen de Duitsche bezettende overheid. In 1942 heb ik met succes het candidaatsexamen in de medicijnen afgelegd. Begin Mei werd het voor mij noodzqkelijk, hed vaderland te verlaten. Na een reis door Belgie en Frankrijk kwam ik op 9 Juli in Spanje aan.

Militaire dienst heb ik niet verricht. In 1937 werd ik te Batavia goedgekeurd. Door mijn verblijf in Nederland eind 1939 is mijn mili- taire lichting eenigen tijd verschoven. Begin 1940 werd ik nogmaals g keurd. De oorlog in Nederland is de oorzaak, dat ik nooit in werkelijk dienst ben geweest, aangezien in in October 1940 waarschijnlijk onder de wapenen had moeten komen.

Ik heb eenmaal getracht, om naar Engeland te komen. De Belgische grens overschreed ik bij Nispen met behulp van grensbewakers. Een vriend te Brussel hielp mij, om bij Heer-Agimont de Fransche grens over te steken. In Parijs werden mij valsche papieren door een Gaullistische organisatie verstrekt. Begin Juli passeerde ik de Pyreneen via St. Grions en Mont Va lliêt Na 5 dagen in de gevangenis te Lerida en alda 10 dagen résidence forcée doorgebracht te hebben, bereikte ik Madrid. Op 28 September vertrok ik naar Portugal.

Praia das Maças, 2 October 1943.

(D. de Moulin)

Biography written by De Moulin in Portugal October 3, 1943, classified 'Zeer geheim' - top secret. The biographies of *Engelandvaarders* were used for background checks.

to Lodewijk was singularly unpleasant. Hoping that it would not take long, we climbed into the airplane.

The airplane, an old Douglas, belonged to KLM, which now only flies two routes: Bristol-Lisbon and Curaçao-Miami and does so like clockwork. The same route is flown by an English company, but while the English company often does not fly if the weather is bad, the Dutch always go and always arrive on the dot. Although it is a Dutch route, the Dutch have little to say about it. Dutchmen who depart from Portugal for England to fight must make a long and dangerous trip by sea, but English women and children who fled England for Canada during the heavy German bombing and who, now that the danger has passed, want to return, must do this by air. No one understands why they don't simply wait until the war is over. Thus the airplane we travelled in transported a lot of little Rothschilds.

It is highly questionable whether our airlines, which before the war were among the largest in the world, will be flown by the Dutch again after the war. We have no equipment and the English and Americans have had an eye on this for a long time already. However, we are bound hand and foot to our biggest allies who will not fail to present us with the bill after the war. We are absolutely powerless against this, thanks to the hopelessly incompetent puppet administration we now have here in London; the few hundred men that make up our army here; our small fleet and even smaller air force (as good as the latter two are). Indeed, the future of the Netherlands looks gloomy. But, we are digressing.

Our flight crew consisted of, amongst others, the well-known [Koene] Parmentier and [Evert] Van Dijk, [the KLM captain during the race from London to Melbourne in 1943, and the first Dutchman to fly over the Atlantic Ocean in 1930, respectively]. We departed at 12:30 am and arrived in Bristol at 6:30 am and after having been interrogated, we were taken under surveillance to London where, for a change, we were interned.

England

A police car was waiting for us at the station in London; we were put into it and the door was securely locked. The vehicle drove us across London to a so-called rest house, a house like so many in London, intended to provide victims provisional shelter against air raids. But this one was specially designed to temporarily accommodate foreign refugees.

The next day we were taken to our definitive 'gaol'; a large building surrounded by a park in one of the suburbs of London. In the past, before the war, it had been an orphanage for the daughters of fallen soldiers and therefore carries the name 'Patriotic School'. We came across men from many different countries here. Everyone who enters England in wartime must first undergo a police investigation before he is allowed to move freely. For the sake of convenience, all of those people are 'condensed' in the school, which you may not leave and from which you are allowed no contact with the outside world and which is under military surveillance. Hendrik spent two and I spent three miserable weeks in that school. They were weeks of intense boredom, too little food and virtually no distraction. Everyone smoked like a chimney so the whole atmosphere was ruined by cigarette smoke. It was a real sensation to be able to smoke endlessly again; neither cigarettes nor bread, for example, has ever been rationed here so everyone made a diligent effort to smoke himself towards bronchitis.

From time to time you were interrogated by the English Intelligence officers who, amongst other languages, also spoke excellent Dutch. On occasion, there was a film on in the evening, but you were usually bored to death. Finally, our imprisonment came to an end and we were taken to 'House Florijs', a special shelter for *Engelandvaarders*. We were interrogated for another two days by the Dutch police and after that, we were finally free. The days that followed were very busy, going to all kinds of agencies like recruitment bureaus, etc.

There are a lot of different Dutch clubs and societies in London, such as the 'Dutch Club', which existed long before the war; the 'Netherlands House', a respectable society funded by the Dutch and English governments, with the aim of improving relations between the two countries; and then also 'Oranjehaven', a small club solely intended for *Engelandvaarders* and given to us as a gift from the queen. A committee representing the different departments is there to advise those who have just arrived about how they can make themselves useful, although as approved, combative Dutchman you are in principle liable to military service, a rule which is only deviated from under very special circumstances and certainly not if you have been placed in the highest level of physical fitness, like I have been.

WELFARE COMMITTEE FOR THE NETHERLANDS FIGHTING FORCES
(Comité ter Bevordering van het Welzyn van Nederlandsche Stryders.)

HONORARY PRESIDENT : H.R.H. PRINCE BERNHARD OF THE NETHERLANDS.

PRESIDENT: W. van de STADT, JR.
HON. SECRETARY : Jhr. J. W. M. SCHORER

EXECUTIVE SECRETARY: P. van ANDEL
Secretariat: 55/7, NEWMAN STREET,
LONDON, W.1

OUR REF.
YOUR REF.

Telephone : Museum 1121

Waarde Landgenoot,

Van harte heeten wij U welkom in ons midden, in Engeland, het land waarheen U gekomen bent om zij aan zij met ons te komen strijden voor de vrijheid van ons geliefd Vaderland.

Enkele dagen zijn noodig voor onderzoek, daar Engeland - de burcht der vrijheid - zijn toegangspoorten angstvallig moet bewaken.

In het bijgaand pakket vindt U het een en ander, dat naar wij vertrouwen welkom zal zijn, terwijl de Hollandsche lectuur en spelen die wij beschikbaar gesteld hebben U den tijd zullen helpen verkorten in Uw tijdelijk verblijf.

Aanvaardt dit pakket als een geste en als een begin van datgene wat wij nog vóor U hopen te doen.

O.Z.O.

Comite ter Bevordering van het Welzijn van
Nederlandsche Strijders.

ALL CORRESPONDENCE TO BE ADDRESSED TO THE SECRETARIAT. CHEQUES AND REMITTANCES TO BE MADE PAYABLE TO : WELFARE COMMITTEE FOR THE NETHERLANDS FIGHTING FORCES.

Welcome letter from the Welfare Committee for the Netherlands Fighting Forces, addressed to all newly arrived *Engelandvaarders*.

Notificatie

Verhoor van: DE MOULIN, Daniel; geboren te Buitenzorg(J
12 September 1919; student; laatstelijk gewoond hebbende
Utrecht, Brigettenstraat No.20a; die Nederland heeft verl
ten op 3 Mei 1943, in Engeland is gearriveerd op 28 Octo
1943 en zich alhier heeft gemeld op 16 November 1943, kom
de van de R.V.P.S.

Vader : Frederik Willem Karel, geboren te Gombong(J
1 Maart 1889; gep.veearts; wonende te Naard
van der Helstlaan No.19.

Moeder : Albertina Augusta Henriette Kroon; geboren
Utrecht, 19 Januari 1893, wonende zelfde ad

Broer : Peter Leonard; oud 20 jaar; geen beroep; is
ondergedoken en thans vermoedelijk in Frankr

Zuster : Eleonora Henriette; oud 22 jaar, verpleegst
Elisabeth Gasthuis te Haarlem.

Ongehuwd

Godsdienst : Nederlandsch-Hervormd.

Politiek : Geen; 9 jaar lid geweest van de Padvinderi

School- : Lagere school, Gymnasium(b) en cand.examen
opleiding medicijnen te Utrecht.

Militaire : Geen.
dienst

Zijn verhoor is een aanvulling op bijlage dezes.

"Ik heb aan illegaal werk gedaan, voornamelijk in de studenten wereld
toen dit door de maatregelen der Duitschers in Mei 1943 afliep, heb ik Ne
land verlaten.
Ik heb Nederland verlaten op 3 Mei 1943 met Mej.KLOESMEYER, in oplei
voor journaliste, oud 18 jaar, wonende te Utrecht en thans verblijvende
Madrid, en M.L.PARREN, oud 24 jaar, student, wonende te Zaltbommel. Wij h
wel eenige adressen, doch de route hebben wij zelf gevonden. Wij hadden
elkaar f.400 bij ons, die wij onderweg gewisseld hebben.
De vriend in Brussel, waar wij 4 Mei 1943 arriveerden, woonde Rue de
Consolation 76, wiens naam ik niet weet. Wij hebben daar 1 nacht geslogen
zij wisselden ons geld in Belgische francs. Aan de Fransche grens is dit
in Fransch geld omgewisseld.
Na het overschrijden der grens bij Heer-Agimont zijn wij per trein g
reisd naar Parijs, alwaar wij op goed geluk een hotelletje, namelijk Mon
vonden, waar wij één nacht geslapen hebben. Den volgenden dag zijn wij d
gegaan naar Sens, alwaar ik in de buurt een kolonie van Nederlandsche bo
wist te vinden. Bij de boer van KEMPEN zijn wij toen een dag of 9 gewees
In Sens stuitten wij toevallig op een lid van een de Gaullistische organ
die ons aan valsche persoonsbewijzen hielp. Ik heb toen in Parijs geprob
een weg te vinden naar het Zuiden en logeerde in het hotel du Nord bij h
station. Begin Juli 1943 zijn wij naar het Zuiden afgezakt en via Toulou

rei

reisden wij naar St.Girons, alwaar wij in een klein hotelletje, Chayenne, onderdak vonden. De eigenaar hield zich bezig met menschen weg te helpen en op 9 Juli 1943 zijn wij de Pyreneeën gepasseerd met 4 Fransche studenten.

Per vliegtuig van Lissabon arriveerde ik op 28 October 1943 in Engeland.

In Madrid hebben Parren en ik een uitvoerig verslag opgemaakt over het verzet in de studentenwereld en later in Lissabon weer bij Mr.Maas Geesteranus. Dit laatste rapport was 7 foliovellen groot. (Dit rapport heeft onzen dienst niet bereikt). Parren is in Portugal, daar hij afgekeurd is voor den militairen dienst.

De burgemeester van Naarden, J.van LEEUWEN, is N.S.B.'er en een Jodenhater.

De burgemeester van Zaltbommel, Jan BOL, die volgens de geruchten vroeger een rijwielstalling heeft gehad, is N.S.B.'er, doch in zijn soort niet kwaad en doet zijn best er iets van te maken.

Het politiepersoneel te Utrecht was over het algemeen niet goed.

Ik weet, dat de advocaten en procureurs zich ook georganiseerd hebben, evenals de artsen en studenten, teneinde zich te kunnen verzetten tegen eventueele komende Duitsche maatregelen. Namen in dit verband heb ik niet gehoord.

De houding van de professoren was over het algemeen zwak, hoewel velen zich later, na het geval der loyaliteitsverklaring, aan onzen kant geschaard hebben. Volgens den heer Poelhekke is alhier aanwezig een volledige verzameling van het illegale studentenblad "De Geuzen", waarin vele namen genoemd worden.

N.S.B.'ers e.d.:

Prof.F.M.J.A.ROELS, te Utrecht, is N.S.B.'er. Zijn zoon, Mr.Roels, is een
                     vooraanstaand figuur in het studentenfront.

dr.F.B.SARIS,   hoofdredacteur van het studentenfront blad, wonende te
                     Leiden.

Ook aan Mr.Maas Geesteranus heb ik een lijst N.S.B.'ers opgegeven."

Een keurige, beschaafde jongeman. Is politiek betrouwbaar.

London, den 18den November

De Luitenant ter Zee II K.M.R.,

Above and opposite: De Moulin's interrogation report by the Dutch Ministry of Justice in London, 18 November 1943. The final judgement about De Moulin was: 'a neat and civilized young man. Politically reliable'.

(A.Wolters.)

Engelandvaarders in front of 'Oranjehaven' (Orange harbor), the Dutch escapees club in London at 23, Hyde Park Place.

So I had the choice between the army, navy and, because I was born in Indonesia, I could also qualify for fast-track training in Australia for the BB, [the colonial civil service]. Hendrik and I also received an offer from the Secret Service.

Now, the last two options were the only possibilities we seriously thought about. The army only consists of 2,000 men and the mood there is very bad. It's always the same thing: hanging about and peeling potatoes under the command of, in part, very incompetent officers. So after extensive consultation, we decided to go to the East Indies for the following reasons: it is of the utmost importance that as many Dutchmen as possible take part in the liberation of the East Indies. Any position in the East Indies Army not taken by a Dutchmen means a vacancy which must be filled by an Englishmen, or worst yet, by an American. One cannot expect the Americans to recapture the East Indies without presenting us with the bill. The conditions under which we are going are very favourable: we will be placed in a training camp for officials of the military authority, that is the administrative officers (this did not happen!). We must go with the troops in order to take administrative control of the recovered area as soon as it has been purged of the enemy. Much, if not everything, depends upon personality and strength of character. When things have calmed down a bit and normal administration can be re-introduced, and once our task has been completed, we will be given the opportunity to graduate in Indology at a university, whereby the training already completed in Australia counts as a bachelor's degree. Moreover, if you are not able to or are unwilling to remain in military service, you will be paid out 25 per cent of the salary you received throughout your service. The chances of promotion are good. We currently have the rank of sergeant; after the training you become a lieutenant. The salary, which is based on the East Indies model, is good. Finally, the work is interesting and very responsible. There are, of course, also drawbacks to this and they are not insignificant. In the first place is the fact that it can take years before we see each other again. And I also realize that I hereby, very worryingly, put my medical career in danger because the chances of picking up my studies after five years is questionable. God only knows how much I would have liked to become a doctor. Sometimes I think it would have been better if I had not gotten involved in resistance work in Holland, had not gone to England, but had calmly gone to Germany when the appeal came. But I know for sure that if I had to do it again, I would do precisely the same thing. I am not your son for nothing!

As I write this, I feel intensely the bond we share and I am proud to have such parents. That is why I know that as unpleasant as this is for all of us, you will understand and accept the steps I have taken. There are situations in which the interests of an individual must be sacrificed for the good of the whole. If it had been Holland, I might have acted differently, but when it comes to liberating the East Indies, it is our duty to fight for it. After the war we will see what happens. I am determined that if I am not needed, I will return to my studies. So do not get rid of my books and instruments, but send them to me as soon as the connections are more or less normal again. In principle, I do not feel like becoming a civil servant and I am wearing a military uniform with even less pleasure, because if there is one thing I have learned is that I have a profound dislike for everything military. But it must be done and I have enough confidence in myself that I know I will be able to achieve something in this area. And so, having carefully considered the advantages and disadvantages, I have signed up with the Royal Dutch East Indies Army 'for the duration of the war and as long as is proves to be necessary'.

Now I will resume the chronicle of events. After having stayed in 'House Florijs' for a couple of days, we were transferred to the barracks of the Netherlands Army's London detachment. I mastered the old army traditions with great virtuosity; I did not come from a military family for nothing! With great dexterity I also got myself out of doing all kinds of awful chores and it took a week before they succeeded in getting me into a uniform; I was usually hiding! Hendrik and I also made sure we were on good terms with the adjutant, an awkward man with thirty years of service behind him and feared by all the recruits.

Shortly after our arrival at the barracks, we were promoted to the rank of petty officer, giving us a lot more freedom and money. At the moment we earn £9 a week, which if you calculate the pound at the official exchange rate of 7,60 guilders, is a lot of money. But you really do need it. London is an expensive city. You can get anything here and mostly without vouchers, but especially where food is concerned, it is expensive and particularly if, like us now, you have relatively little to do and are waiting for your ship to set sail. It all almost didn't happen. During my inspection for the East Indies, my blood sedimentation levels were not good and they suspected tuberculosis. So, early in January, I was sent to the hospital for a week of observation. That was anything but fun; the food was appalling and I was fussed over and mothered by a whole bunch of women. All the nurses felt sorry for the poor little boy that lay there, far from home, so I didn't have a life.

After a few weeks in the barracks, we were given leave to live on our own and Hendrik and I went to live in 'House OZO', [Oranje Zal Overwinnen: the house Orange and the Netherlands will overcome]. The house [was founded] upon the queen's initiative as a hotel for Dutch soldiers and so on, who had to be in London temporarily. It is nicely decorated and because we get on well with the manager, Mrs Knappert, we feel very much at home.

Incidentally, London is an unpleasant city and very dirty. Your shirt collar is black in no time, you have black nails and apart from a few exceptions, I find there is nothing beautiful about it. The city has been damaged greatly by the air raids and although not over any great expanses, you do regularly see a gap where a housing block once stood. The City, in particular, is rather badly damaged. It is difficult to amuse yourself in London. Anything to do with entertainment is very expensive. You have excellent theatrical performances, and very good concerts, but it is too expensive to go to them regularly.

Hendrik and I soon picked up a few really nice girls with whom we go out regularly. It is not difficult to come by girlfriends; the women here are rather cheap and the morality is disappointing. But even

with the "better" English girls, your chances as a foreigner are very good. The average Englishman is rather ill-mannered when it comes to women, so if you treat them with some consideration, you can look forward to great popularity amongst them. The other day I went to a ball organized by the medical assistants from the hospital. I have never seen such a collection of beautiful girls together in all my life and I have never felt so popular. They literally fought over me and each one was even prettier than the next.

I do not take much part in Dutch society here in London. A Dutch colony abroad is always boring. We live in a mini-state here and regularly speak with ministers, generals and other high-level personalities (I mean people). The queen, too, is far more visible here than in Holland. Shortly after we arrived, we had an audience with her. She was very simple and most interested and well-informed about everything. It is truly a blessing that we have her as queen. You can tell that the current situation weighs her down; she has aged tremendously.

I am a regular with minister [Gerrit] Bolkestein. I often pop into his room, without having asked in advance. I have a lot to do with him, as minister of education, in connection with my attempt to unite the students present here in England as part of the International Council of Students in England, to ensure together that the intellect of those students does not get lost in the mind-numbing life of the military, by organizing lectures, concerts, making books and literary journals available, and so forth. I do not know if I will succeed. Lodewijk, who will probably bring you this book, will tell you more about this. Still, life here is very educational; for example, you learn that you can talk with a minister with the same ease as a simple soldier.

Our immediate future is unsure; the Dutch East Indies detachment departs next week to a military camp in England, from which we deduce that for the time being, there is little chance we will depart. I don't necessarily need to go, for health reasons. It appears they hadn't found anything and the blood sediment is once more normal so that we have attributed my temporarily low levels to undernourishment. Mrs Kappert is so very kind to me and she follows me around all day with glasses of milk and sandwiches. I also regularly lie under sunlamps. This and that means that I currently feel great. But because I have to undergo a blood test again next week, it means I must stay here for the time being. So Hendrik and I will soon part ways. I hope to see Lodewijk soon who, word has it, is already at the Patriotic

Farewell picture from Hendrik to Daniël: 'We are not afraid (at least, not very much so). Hendrik'

School. But everything is very uncertain now and hangs in the air. Hence, for the near future, I will end this book with a big question mark. I am confident about the future in the longer term. I have been so well helped by unknown forces so far, that I trust that they will do so in the future too. And what more could one want?

London, 16 February 1944

Daan.

This book should arrive in a sealed condition.

Escaping Occupied Europe

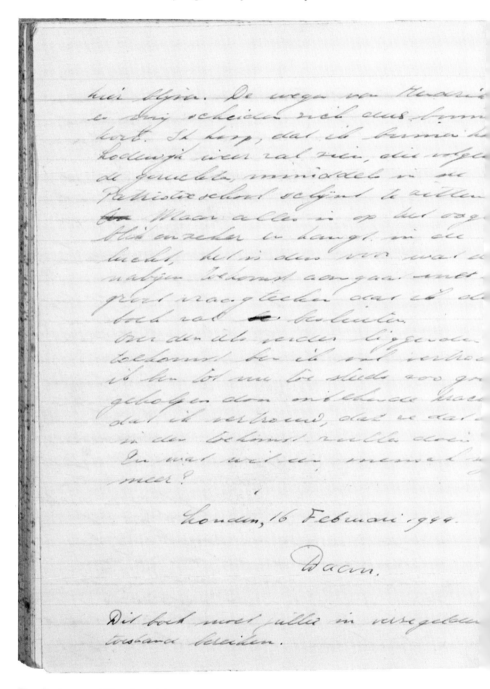

The final pages of the chronicle.

122

Georganië.

Spanje

Portugal

Engeland

 Aanschouw gijle voorstelling van mijn
haargroei gedurende de twee maan-
den volgende op het verblijf in
de gevangenis.

Reception of *Engelandvaarders* by Queen Wilhelmina at Palace Het Loo, 17 August 1948.

Chapter 4

After the *Engelandvaart*

At the time De Moulin completed his travelogue, he had decided to serve in the Dutch colonies, but his 'immediate future was unclear'. He gave his manuscript to Lodewijk Parren with the request to hand it over to his parents. Daniël awaited what would come, 'confident about the future in the longer term'.

Lodewijk had just arrived two days earlier at the Patriotic School. He had initially been rejected for military service, and therefore had to stay behind in Portugal. With the help of Daniël he managed to secure a job in London and was finally allowed to travel to England. Lodewijk finished his *Engelandvaart* and arrived at the Patriotic School on 14 February 1944. However, Daan and Lodewijk never met in London.

As an enlisted soldier, De Moulin was assigned to the infantry of the Royal Netherlands East Indies Army (KNIL) and promoted to sergeant. Though he expected that, 'for the time being, there is little chance we will depart', he couldn't have been more wrong: he set sail on 18 February 1944 and, with a stopover in Durban (South Africa), arrived in Australia in early May 1944.

In the meantime, Parren was released from the Patriotic School and reunited with De Moulin's brother, Peter, and their year club member, Armand Berg. Both had made it safely to London. Whereas Peter's *Engelandvaart* went smoothly, Armand encountered more danger. He was betrayed in France by a hotelier and arrested, after which he ended up in the Noé concentration camp, located between Toulouse and Garbonne. During a nighttime air raid warning he managed to escape and successfully continued his *Engelandvaart*.

In London, Parren worked for the displaced persons department of the Dutch Ministry of Social Affairs at 1 St. James's Street. He assisted with the preparation of the safe return home of Dutchmen in liberated France following D-Day. Parren also joined the board of the Dutch Student Association in England, which Daan had started. In this

Daniël and Hendrik on an elephant in the Valley of a Thousand Hills, South Africa.

The envelope, opened by a German (left) and Allied (right) examiner.

Peter de Moulin, Lodewijk Parren and Armand Berg in London, 19 August 1944.

capacity he held a so-called "Students Talk", which was broadcast by the BBC for Radio Oranje on 14 May 1944.

At the end of March or early April, Parren received a letter from his mother. It was sent from the Netherlands the same day De Moulin finished his travelogue and arrived in Portugal on 6 March 1944; three weeks after Lodewijk had left for London. The letter, which had been opened by a German and an Allied examiner, read: 'Jos is working in Paris for the German Wehrmacht and has a secret address'. It confirmed the suspicion Daan wrote about in his travelogue, but hadn't taken seriously:

I filled [Josje] *with drinks and subjected her to something resembling a cross-examination. Various people had warned me about her; she was supposedly Gestapo. However, there was no indication whatsoever for this [...] Indeed, the fact that she had received a return visa for France was a strange thing. She had worked in Paris in the past and, although she had a good job in the Netherlands, she now wanted to look for something in France again. And, in fact, succeeded.*

So, although not a Gestapo agent, Josje did work for the Germans. She had several jobs in France and the Netherlands, for the Wehrmacht, the Dutch-German *Kulturgemeinschaft* (cultural community) and for a short time she allegedly even worked as an announcer for German

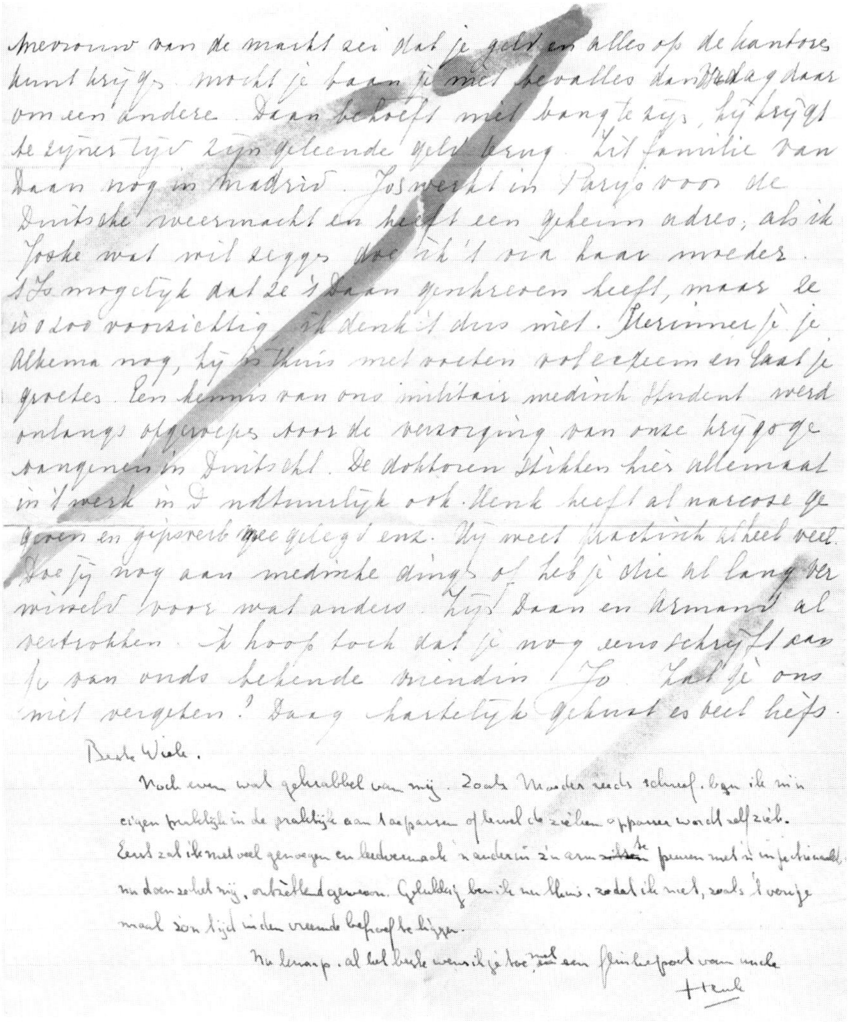

[handwritten letter in Dutch]

Second page of the letter from Lodewijk's mother with the information about Josje, sent on 16 February 1944.

television in France (*Fernsehsender Paris*). At the end of the war, she was private secretary to the Rotterdam *Kreisleiter* - the Nazi Party political rank of county leader. According to her own statement, this was not out of sympathy with the German cause, but because the jobs were well paid and the food was good.

Parren flew to France on 14 November 1944 to assist with the repatriation of Dutch refugees in Western Europe. While in France he helped with the registration and medical checkups of displaced persons.

P 74. (Parren)   *uitreil. 8/8 44 — 2356/P99)*
Afschrift   MOST SECRET.   13

FROM : Parren, Gamenke Str. 4, Zeitbonnel, Holland.

TO: SleaHor Don Parren
       U.K.

Translated Extracts:- "Henk came home on January 10 for 4 weeks
leave. He had trouble with his lungs in D. and is now having
treatment in UTRECHT from specialists, But they have no room
there to take him in yet so he is still at home......We are now
quietly awaiting a verifying doctor from the NIJMEGEN Labour
Bureau under whose authority he is. In D. conditions were very good
and the work was nice which was a great comfort to us,
but it is a pity now about this illness................DAAN'S
family is still in MDRID. JOS is working in Paris for the
German WEHRMACHT and has a secret address. If I want to say
anything to JOSKE I do it through her mother. She may have given
it to DAAN, but I don't think so, she is so careful. Do you
remember ALKEMA, he is home with eczema all over his feet, and
sends you his greetings. An aquaintance of ours a military
medical student was called up recently to look after our prisoners
of war in Germany. The doctors here are overwhelmed with
work, in Germany too, of course. HENK has already given anaes-
thetics and applied plaster bandages. He knew a lot of the
practical side."

Bijlage: 5.

Voor eensluidend afschrift,
Het wnd. Hoofd van Afdeeling II
van het Departement van Justitie.

A. Dees.

Translation of fragments of the letter by an Allied examiner.

Transports of large groups of civilians were not possible yet as the
train capacity in liberated France was needed for transporting troops,
weapons and military vehicles. Once they were given permission by
the Americans, Parren travelled back and forth by train with groups of
displaced persons from France to the Netherlands as a medical officer.

Meanwhile, De Moulin received his military training at Camp Columbia
in Wacol, near Brisbane. He was assigned to the Melbourne Detachment,
and from New Guinea, took part in the Allied offensive against Japan.

De Moulin at Camp Columbia in Wacol, near Brisbane.

MINISTERIE
VAN SOCIALE ZAKEN

(Netherlands Government)
(Department of Social Affairs)

Tel.: Gro. 4181

32/16

ARLINGTON HOUSE,

ARLINGTON STREET,

LONDON, S.W.1

10th November

This is to certify that Mr. M. L.
Parren who is an accredited official of the Royal
Netherlands Government is proceeding to France to
take up medical duties for the Netherlands
Repatriation Mission, in accordance with the
Provisions of the Bilateral Agreement between the
Government of France and the Royal Netherlands
Government concluded on the 20th September, 1944 .

G. F. Ferwerda
Netherlands Commissioner for
Repatriation.

Work permit for Lodewijk Parren.

Because of his background as a medical student, he was given the task of
supplying the army and the population in liberated areas with medical
supplies. On 15 November 1944, he was honorably discharged from the
KNIL and appointed as second lieutenant in the Infantry Reserves for
special services. After the Japanese surrender in August 1945, De Moulin
fulfilled this role in Australia, New Guinea and Java and, after reuniting
with Armand Berg, provided emergency supplies for recently liberated
Japanese camps and other areas that had been affected by the war.

After the war

On 26 June 1945 Parren finally returned home, though not without having to overcome a final barrier. Being a civilian and not having the right papers, the Allies didn't allow him to cross the Meuse river. He therefore had to charter a rowing boat and crossed the river illegally, after which he borrowed a bike and cycled home. He was reunited with his family and soon afterwards handed Daan's travelogue to De Moulin's parents.

Almost a year later, on 18 June 1946, more than three years after the start of his journey, De Moulin finally set foot again on Dutch soil. He had left the Dutch East Indies on 23 May 1946 on the MS *Tegelberg* and was demobilized and reunited with his family and year club members, who had all survived the war.

The only person De Moulin and Parren never met again was Kloesje. While in Spain, Kloesje did not receive a visa for England because, as a woman, she was deemed to be of no relevance to the war effort. When their ways parted in Madrid on 29 September 1943, Kloesje therefore stayed and moved in with the Dutch acting consul, Schölvinck, with whom she started a relationship. She was repatriated to the Netherlands on 11 September 1945, but went back to Spain soon after. Schölvinck and Kloesje moved to Caïro, Egypt in 1948 and to Beira, in Portuguese East Africa (now Mozambique) in 1951. From 1954 onwards they lived in Southern Rhodesia (Zimbabwe) where they married on 2 May 1961. Kloesje worked as a librarian and taught physical education

Kloesje in Cairo with her first-born, Roy, 1948.

Kloesje in later life in Napa, 1990.

at the Nagle House Convent. In 1980 she started working at a building society and afterwards became assistant credit controller for the same farmers' co-operation that her husband worked for. Kloesje passed away in Marondera, Zimbabwe on 21 May 2001.

Back in the Netherlands, De Moulin and Parren tried to continue their normal life. Both resumed their medical studies and became active again in the student community. They helped with rebuilding the Unitas S.R. student association and had various roles in committees and acted in plays. Daan also founded a literary circle where he met English student Jannie Luit (whom he married in 1952).

Also trying to pick up her normal life was Josje. Immediately after the liberation she switched sides and was a nurse with the *Binnenlandse Strijdkrachten* (Dutch Domestic Forces). She was apprehended, however, and sentenced to several years internment due to her confidential relations with Germans, for aiding the enemy, and for espionage. Nonetheless, after a just few months she was released. Her marriage to a high-level BS (*Binnenlandse Strijdkrachten*) employee in August 1945 and the positive testimony given by De Moulin and his parents about how she had helped Daniël, Lodewijk and Kloesje during the war may have helped. Josje became a physiotherapist after the war.

133

De Moulin with scepter as protocol officer in front of the procession marking the 35th anniversary of the Unitas S.R. student association, November 1946.

Josephina Wertz in later life.

In 1949, De Moulin passed his final medical exams and started his training as a general surgeon in the city of Tilburg. From 1958 to 1964, he was the chief surgeon at the St. Liduina Hospital in Boxtel.

In 1964 he obtained his PhD with honors for his thesis on medicine in the Middle Ages. In the years that followed he taught at, amongst other places, Johns Hopkins University in Baltimore. In 1971, De Moulin resumed his surgical practice in Boxtel and became lecturer in the History of Medicine at the Catholic University of Nijmegen (now Radboud University). In 1978 De Moulin was appointed

Daniël de Moulin as a surgeon in the early 1950s.

as a full professor. During his scientific career he authored a large number of articles, chapters and books, both in Dutch and in English.

In 1987, De Moulin received the Gold Medal of Honor from the Dutch Society of Medicine. The following year, in April 1988, De Moulin was badly injured during a robbery in the United States. As a result, the last years of his life were marked by disability. In 1989 he said farewell as a professor with a symposium about medicine in the Dutch East Indies. Daniël de Moulin died in Boxtel on 9 February 2002, at the age of 82.

Lodewijk Parren passed his final exams in 1950 and started his training as a urologist. After his graduation in May 1957, he started his practice in Enschede. After his retirement in 1983 he lived a quiet life due to the passing away of his wife in 1984 and his diminishing eyesight. In May 2006 he was the guest of honor during the presentation of the Dutch edition of this book. Parren passed away that same year, on 26 December.

For their activities during the Second World War, De Moulin and Parren received several awards: the *Verzetsherdenkingskruis* (Resistance Memorial Cross) and the *Kruis van Verdienste* (Cross of Merit). De Moulin also received the *Oorlogsherinneringskruis* (War Commemoration Cross), and the *Ereteken voor Orde en Vrede* (the Medal of Order and Peace).

Daniël de Moulin in later life.

Lodewijk Parren in later life.

Appendix I – The French on *Les Hollandais*

Philippe Raichlen ·

1 – Meeting *Les Hollandais*
A sudden noise in nearby bushes. Alert. No, it was the rest of the convoy; two pale, thin men and a poorly dressed young girl. They introduced themselves: Daniel (Daan) (de) Moulin, Louis (Lodewijk) Parren, Roel (Kloesie) Kloesmeyer. Pursued by the Gestapo since they had left Utrecht, they had crossed three borders illegally, that of Holland, Belgium, near Lille and then, finally, the forbidden line in the north of France. Living a precarious existence in Paris and being increasingly pursued, they finally reached St Girons with no food, no money, no papers. To survive, they had had to eat green wheat from fields, after attempting to cook it on a small fire. They were now exhausted: so close to the final frontier, would they fall into the hands of the enemy? Roel, with her naive young Dutch face, had horrible memories of the tortures she had seen, which had been forced upon her during the nine months of jail there. But in the midst of their anguish they found the strength to smile, to joke, and we, with our bags well packed with food, maps and money, wanted to pretend that we were heroes!

2 – Climbing the Pyrenees
Louis Parren, who was weaker and looked as if he might have tuberculosis, collapsed and begged us to leave him on the roadside. We had to hold him up with the strength of our wrists and then it needed two of us to carry him. The two other Dutchmen joked at every fall, but with the burning desire to overcome all difficulties. And I, who was last in the line, I was watching these poor figures that did not stop falling into the darkness. To see so much suffering made me stronger: was it misplaced pride or a sense of my responsibilities? I felt that an unspecified duty rested on my shoulders. What that was precisely, however, I would not have been able to say.

3 – Lérida Prison

The parlour. A young and fresh pink-faced girl with red hair. But here is Roel! 'You see, the first thing I did was to go to a hairdresser! In Paris I had my hair dyed black, because red is too light. But now, libertad! And then I went to the governor of the province. He received me in his parlour, a real gentleman. Your release was given to me all at once. "Claro que sí, Señorita. Mañana por la mañana" (Of course, miss, tomorrow morning). The next day, nothing. The next day, nothing. The next day, nothing. I returned: same story. A thousand excuses. "Mañana por la mañana." And they gave me my safe passage to Madrid. Ah, but I will stay here! And I harassed the governor of Lerida. There you go.'

We all laughed like crazy. And finally, finally, we went through that iron-studded door. 'Coño I will return mañana por la mañana!'

The street was too narrow for our joy. We were walking on clouds. How could we go so rapidly from a nightmare to the most unexpected happiness? Bourcart leapt into the air. Escande smiled at all the señoras. I breathed the night air, deeply.

Roel lead us to the Cuatro Naciones, a hotel for "foreigners passing through". Good dinner with the three Dutch. A waiter served us good spicy dishes with olive oil. The scent of Spain.

4 - Gratitude and farewell

Secretary Povida came to honour the Belgians with his gracious presence. Roel accompanied him faithfully, defending our interests. She knew exactly what she wanted. If she had left us here, we could have stayed a very long time. The secretary was enchanted with her. What a strange girl!

Lavish meals, the Belgian national anthem, swing, singing, the Marseillaise, rough and heady wine. Oppressive heat in this hole where the sun beats down. Povida announced our forthcoming release.

We took Roel aside. She had been so good to us. As a farewell gift, our team gave her a ring brought by Hugues, with a diamond, in memory of all of us. She left and we never saw her again.

Hugues Bohn

1 – Meeting *Les Hollandais*

Louis: tall, blond , very "Dutch-looking", a medical student.
Daniel: mixed-race of Indian and Dutch descent, a medical student.
Roel: extremely Dutch-looking, a journalist, 18 years old.

They left Holland three months ago, running away from the Gestapo. They went through Belgium, where their money had been confiscated. Then they reached Paris where they lived for two months, changing hotels every few days, and eating one day in three. They stayed in Saint-Girons for three days with no money, so no food or a roof [over their heads], *even though last night it rained cats and dogs. They had very poor equipment; a coat on their arm, low shoes, with torn soles. And they were exhausted. Arriving in Alos, Louis fainted and we had to pull him up, then push and support him, to carry him up to the barn...*

2 – Climbing the Pyrenees
Louis and Roel struggled to walk. Roel had real guts. She walked almost barefoot on the rocks and stones.

3 – Lérida Prison
10 July: The two Dutch doctors go to work at the prison's infirmary. Roel was on probation in the town, she was very busy at the Dutch consulate in an attempt to free them (13 July), and she tried to do the same to free us ....

   17 July: We were called, we are free! Roel waited for us outside the prison. She was the one who got us out through her personal intervention via the Dutch governor's secretary. Dinner with the three Dutch people was very cheerful.

4 - Gratitude and farewell
21 July: Belgium's national bank holiday. Roel and the Dutch secretary were invited. They left rather tipsy... Very touching farewells, Roel due to leave tomorrow for Madrid.

Robert Bourcart

1 – Lérida Prison
An astounding noise buzzed under my temples: 'we are free, immediate departure.'

   A lightning bolt falling three yards away from me would not have left me more impressed. But how can one believe this sudden happiness? I also had to hear this reality shouted out loud to believe it. With my pack on my back, I almost tumbled down the stairs headfirst and, two minutes later, I was outside on the other side of the terrible door, overwhelmed with joy and squeezing the hands of our liberator, Roel, the Dutchwoman from the Pyrenees. In gratitude to us, she had remained in Lérida for a week, demanding our liberation from the Governor twice a day. Not having been able to obtain it, she had just seduced the Secretary General, who, as a good Spaniard, had granted her all her requests the day after their first evening together. What the most powerful recommendations could not have obtained, a simple girl had just offered to me, as well as to my four mountain companions. The moral of story: a good deed always finds its reward.

Appendix II – Index of names

Included in this index of names are persons and organizations that appear in and are relevant to De Moulin's travelogue, about which we know more than De Moulin mentions in the original manuscript itself.

Bakkes, H.T.F. (Harry), (1909-1882)
Herman Wientjes's associate.

Berg, A.M. (Armand), (1921-2006)
Pharmacy student. Member of the year club *Inter nos* and Fiscus in the College of Ephors. He fled to England with Wim Westbroek and Johan Wilderinck, both members of Unitas S.R. They were betrayed in France by a hotelier. Westbroek was able to escape but Berg and Wilderinck were arrested and ended up in Noé concentration camp, located between Toulouse and Garbonne. During a nighttime air raid alarm, they were able to escape and reached England anyway. Berg left for New Guinea where he worked with Daniël de Moulin.

Bohn, Hugues, (1921-2011)
Student at the Colonial Administration School. He decided to escape from France to avoid forced labour in Germany. He reached North Africa in November 1943, along with Philippe Raichlen and Emile Escande. As an officer of the *Corps Expéditionnaire Français*, he participated in the battles of the Italy Campaign, and in the landing at Provence in 1944. After the war, he worked in French Indochina (Saigon, Vietnam), and back in France, later worked for the family business, a printing company called Berger-Levrault.

Bourcart, Robert, (1919-2011)
Law student. In 1943, he decided to interrupt his studies to join the resistance Free French Forces, led by General de Gaulle in North Africa. He reached Casablanca, Morocco, on 21 October 1943 after having escaped France. Shortly afterwards, he enlisted in the General Leclerc Division. The British Special Operations Executive (SOE) trained him to become an expert at

guerrilla warfare and parachuted him into the Provence region on 17 April 1944. He led a group of armed fighters in the Rhone Valley and took part in various acts of guerrilla warfare. In the spring of 1945, he enlisted voluntarily so that he could fight in French Indochina, thereby helping to restore colonial rule there (this was the final step required for the Liberation of France). He was parachuted into Laos and after months of guerrilla warfare, he moved back to France in April 1946. He was a French Colonial Administrator in Guinea from 1948 until 1951 and then in Dakar, Senegal, from 1952 until 1959, where he obtained his law degree doctorate. He moved back to France at the end of 1959.

Bolkestein, G. (Gerrit), (1871-1956)
Minister of Education, Art and Science from 1939 to 1945, in the cabinets of De Geer II and Gerbrandy I, II and III. From London (in 1943), he appealed to students not to sign the Loyalty Declaration.

Buth, Maartje Aagje (1922-?), see: Kempen, H.P. (Huig Pieter) van.

College of Ephors
Board of Resistance of the Unitas S.R Student Association. Formed to safeguard all association affairs in wartime and the preparation of the re-establishment thereof after the war. The college was installed on 15 May 1942 and consisted of Daniël De Moulin, Lodewijk Parren, Armand Berg and Wim Heirsch.

Dijk, Evert van, (1893-1986)
The first Dutchman to fly over the Atlantic Ocean in 1930. Flew Daniël de Moulin from Lisbon to London on 27 October 1943.

Escande, Emile, (1921-1999)
A student at the Colonial Administration School, with Hugues Bohn.

Gaillard, J.W. (Jan Willem), (1920-2002)
A student of Dutch-East Indian Law. Pseudonym for Henry Lons, nicknamed Hendrikje. Gaillard worked undercover in the Netherlands for an espionage group. When the Gestapo began looking for him, he fled the Netherlands. He was arrested in the Pyrenees and detained for half a year in Camp Miranda de Ebro, Spain. After his release, he reached Madrid the end of September and a month later travelled to England with Daniël de Moulin.

Heirsch, W.H. (Wim), (1920-1959)
Pharmacy student. Member of year club *Inter nos* and Commissioner in the College van Ephors

Hubers, J.G. (Jan), (1924-1993)
Photography student in Hengelo. Amongst other things, he provided the passport photos accompanying false documents. He himself says that he also escorted French prisoners of war and Allied pilots in the Netherlands who were on their way south. To avoid being sent to work in Germany, he left for France with the help of Herman Wientjes, who was from his own home town. He became a shepherd at the Van Kempen farm in Sens. Hubers helped Daniël de Moulin and his friends get into contact with La Croix and Herman Wientjes.

House Florys
A shelter in London for *Engelandvaarders* rented by the Dutch government. It could house approximately fifteen people.

Inter nos
Unitas year club from 1939 onwards consisting of Daniël de Moulin, Lodewijk Parren, Armand Berg, Wim Heirsch, Cees van Montfoort and Carel van Mourik.

Kempen, H.P. (Huig Pieter) van, (1914-?)
Farmer at 'La Goujauderie' in Les Clérimois. Married to Maartje Aagje Buth (1922-?), the sister of a friend of Rolande Kloesmeijer's. Shortly after Daniël de Moulin and his friends' stay, on 9 June 1943, Adriana Johanna was born.

Kloesmeijer, R.C. (Rolande Catarine), (1924-2001)
Journalism student. Nicknamed Kloesje. Said she was sought by the German police because of her alleged communist sympathies. Kloesje went into hiding with the De Moulin family in Naarden, who knew her via her cousin Cees van Montfoort, a fraternity friend of Daniël De Moulin's. She fled to Spain with De Moulin and Lodewijk Parren by way of Belgium and France. She did not get a visa for England because, as a woman, she was of no relevance to the war effort and therefore stayed in Spain until her repatriation on 11 September 1945. Kloesje got involved with the acting Dutch consul of Madrid, Felix Theodoor Schölvinck, with whom she moved to Egypt, Portuguese East Africa (Mozambique) and Rhodesia and married on 2 May 1961 in Salisbury, Rhodesia (now Zimbabwe).

KNIL
The Royal Netherlands East Indies Army, the Dutch colonial army that was founded in 1830 in the Dutch East Indies.

Littaur, H.W.M. (Heinz), (1900-1978)
Director of the Bijenkort (a well-known department store in the Netherlands) during the early years of the war. He fled to Switzerland in 1940.

Moulin, D. (Daniël) de, (1919-2002)
Medical student. Member of the fraternity *Inter nos* and President of the College of Ephors. De Moulin fled to England in 1943 with Lodewijk Parren and Rolande Kloesmeijer.

Moulin, P. (Peter) de, (1923-2003)
Daniël de Moulin's brother and member of Unitas S.R. Daniël did not want Peter to join him on his *Engelandvaart* because he wanted to distribute the respective dangers and he also felt four people was too many. Peter therefore left for England a month and a half after his brother Daniël and made it to England.

Moulin, F.W.K. (Frederik) de, (1898-1957)
Daniël and Peter de Moulin's father. A veterinarian in the East Indies at the Veterinary School; later a professor in Utrecht.

Moulin, A.A.H. (Albertina) de, (1898-1993)
Daniël and Peter de Moulin's mother. Violinist.

Naeff, P.C. (Pieter), (1903-1962)
Assistant to J.W. Kolkman at the Office Néerlandais (Dutch Office) in Perpignan. When everything there closed, he left (early in 1943) to fulfill a similar position in Lyon. He worked on an escape route for *Englandvaarders*. When he was sought by the Gestapo, he left for Switzerland where he became a repatriation officer in 1945.

Oom, Jan, (1920-1944)
Dutch millionaire. Oom was training to become a Marconist [telegraph or radio operator], first in the Netherlands and later in Germany. He came back dressed in an SS uniform but soon became part of the resistance. When this was brought to an end, he escaped to Paris. From 1943 onwards, he occasionally helped refugees and could be found at the Hotel Oria, the centre of the Dutch black market in Paris. The day before Daniël de Moulin arrived and subsequently fled Paris, a raid took place. Oom was arrested by the Germans and transported to Buchenwald, where he was killed shortly afterwards.

Parmentier, Koene Dirk, (1904-1948)
KLM captain during the race from London to Melbourne in 1934. He flew Daniël de Moulin from Lisbon to London on 27 October 1943.

Parren, M.L. (Lodewijk), (1919-2006)
Medical student. Member of year club *Inter nos* and Secretary of the College of Ephors. Parren fled to England with Daniël De Moulin and Rolande Kloesmeijer in 1943.

Post, L.J. (Leo), (1915-1944)
Very likely the Dutch priest. Post was the Abbé in Mérobert, a small place south of Paris. He was active in escorting Dutch refugees, but was betrayed. He was arrested on the way to Pau in October 1943. Via Buchenwald, he ended up in Mauthaussen. He did not survive the concentration camp.

Raichlen, Philippe, (1920-1949)
Political Science student. He decided to escape from France to avoid forced labour in Germany. As he wanted to fight openly in uniform, he decided to enlist in the French Army in North Africa. With his cousin Hugues Bohn and friend Emile Escande, he reached North Africa in November 1943. Philippe fought as a paratrooper to free the east of France in the winter of 1944-45. For this, he was awarded the "Croix de Guerre". Philippe committed suicide at the age of 28.

Royal Patriotic School (R.P.S.)
At the outbreak of war, Security Control officers at ports were responsible for collecting military information from aliens entering the UK. The collection of this information was initially the responsibility of MI5 officers, but in May 1941, MI9 became responsible for the 'Ia' interrogation of those aliens who were sent to the London Reception Centre. In January 1941 the premises of the Royal Victoria Patriotic School, Trinity Road, Wandsworth, London SW18, were taken over by the Internment Camps Division of the Home Office, and opened on 8 January 1941 for the reception of aliens and refugees of Allied and friendly countries. It was known as the 'London Reception Centre'. Essentially, civilians were interrogated as a sifting process for useful military information, and to identify enemy agents (political agents); also, individuals may be 'approached' for their suitability to act as Allied agents (for example Norwegian fishermen). As with military prisoners of war, individuals were interrogated at ports and then transferred to R.P.S. Before the end of 1944, the staff was reduced and after the new year, officers, other ranks and civilian staff were released for work elsewhere. The section was finally disbanded on 31 May 1945.

Schölvinck, Felix Theodoor (1904-1967)
Administrator at the shipping company Koninklijke Nederlandse Maatschappij voor Havenwerken and acting Dutch consul in Madrid. Was married to Margaretha Elisabeth le Cosquino de Bussy when he met Rolande Kloesmeijer (Kloesje). He moved with Kloesje to Egypt, where he

was responsible for management of the Edfina Barrage. He later moved to Portuguese East Africa (Mozambique) and Rhodesia where, after his official divorce in 24 June 1960, he married Kloesje on 2 May 1961 in Salisbury, Rhodesia (now Zimbabwe). He was an administrator in Marandellas Rhodesië, where he passed away on 18 December 1967.

Soutif, Jolande, (?-?)
A friend of Daniël de Moulin and Josje. Lived in Paris under the name Evelyn.

Unitas Studiosorum Rheno-Traiectina, (1911-)
Mixed student association in Utrecht, established on 21 November 1911.

Unitasfluitje (*literally*: Unitas whistle)
The first line of the Unitas S.R. corps song entitled *Studenten juicht en jubelt* (Students cheer and rejoice).

Wertz, J. (Josephina), (1919-)
Worked for the Wehrmacht in a variety of positions in Paris during the war, and for a short time worked as a television broadcaster in French Television. At the end of the war she was private secretary to the Rotterdam Kreisleiter - the Nazi Party political rank of county leader- and directly after that as liberation nurse with the *Binnenlandse Strijdkrachten* (Dutch Domestic Forces)! After the war, she was sentenced to a few years internment due to her confidential relations with Germans, for helping the enemy and even for espionage, but was released a few months later. Her marriage to a high-level BS (*Binnenlandse Strijdracht*) employee and the positive statements given by De Moulin's parents about how she helped Daan, Lodewijk and Kloesje may have helped.

Westbroek, Wim, (1923-?)
Fled to England with Armand Berg and Johan Wilderink, both members of Unitas S.R. They were betrayed in France by a hotelier, but Westbroek succeeded in escaping. Later he was apprehended and taken to the transit camp in Compiègne. From there, on 29 January 1944, he was transported to Buchenwald concentration camp (prisoner number Bu 44308). Westbroek survived the camp and returned to Utrecht. He became a naturalized citizen of New Zealand in 1967 and he was last heard of in Taupo, Waikato in 1981.

Wientjes, H.J. (Herman), (1915-1999)
Harry Bakkes's sidekick. Stayed alternately in the Netherlands and Paris during the war, amongst other things, as a black marketeer. He was arrested several times by the Germans for *Feindbegünstigung* (aiding the enemy). In his role as *Transportführer* (transport leader) he accompanied labourers on

their travels through Europe. He was also able to help *Engelandvaarders* by giving them blank travel documents.

Wilderink, F.J. (Johan), (1923-1989)

Distributor of resistance paper *Vrij Nederland*. He fled to England with Armand Berg and Wim Westbroek, both members of Unitas S.R. He was betrayed in France by a hotelier. Westbroek escaped but Wilderinck and Berg were arrested and ended up in Noé concentration camp, located between Toulouse and Garbonne. During the nighttime air alarm, they managed to escape and reach England.

Bibliography

Primary

Moulin, D. de, *Aan mijn opvolger*. Utrecht, 1942. At: het Utrechts Archief, Utrecht. Collection Unitas 780, inventarisnummer 100.

Moulin, D. de, *Korte beschrijving van de gebeurtenissen die zich hebben afgespeeld in de week van 13-19 December 1942*. At: het Utrechts Archief, Utrecht. Collection Unitas 780, inventarisnummer 100.

Moulin, D. de & Parren, M.L., *Het georganiseerde studentenverzet in Nederland*. Praia das Maçãs, 1943. At: Nationaal Archief, Den Haag. Ministerie van Justitie te Londen inventarisnummer 12132.

Moulin, D. de & Parren, M.L., *Over verzetsgeest en verzetsactie in Nederland*. Praia das Maçãs, 1943. At: Nationaal Archief, Den Haag. Ministerie van Justitie te Londen, inventarisnummer 12132.

Moulin, D. de, *Kroniek van de lotgevallen van Daniël de Moulin tijdens diens reis naar Engeland in het jaar 1943*. At: Nationaal Archief, Den Haag. Collection losse aanwinsten betreffende de Tweede Wereldoorlog (1939-1945). Toegang 2.22.17, inventarisnummer 21.

Moulin, D. de, 'Van de onzen in de vreemde'. In: *Vivos Voco*, jaargang 20 (1946), nummer 11, p. 4.

Moulin, D. de, Parren, M.L. e.a., *U.S.R. en het studentenverzet. 'All wars are civil wars'*. Utrecht, 1947. At: Utrechts Archief, Utrecht. Collection Utrechts Verzet 650, inventarisnummer 16, Collection Unitas 780, inventarisnummer 1125.

Moulin, D. de, 'Utrechtse herinneringen'. In: *Vivos Voco*, jaargang 62 (1985), nummer 8, pp. 13-16.

Parren, M.L., 'Algemeen verslag. Van Juni 1941 tot eind April 1943'. In: *U.S.R. Boek* 1946. Utrecht, Unitas Studiosorum Rheno-Traiectina, 1946. pp. 59-67.

Parren, M.L., Questionnaire Engelandvaarders by A.M.F. Dessing.

Parren, M.L., interview by H. Faber & P. Stolk. Enschede, 30 oktober 2004 and 6 augustus 2005.

Parren, M.L., spoken bibliography/memoires and personal files. 1994/1995. At: family Lodewijk Parren.

Secondary

Berg, A.M., interview by H. Faber & P. Stolk. Rijswijk, 22 November 2004.

Bruineman, J., *Metterdaad. Vijf jaar onderdrukking en verzet in Bussum*. Stichting Uitgeverij Walden, pp. 43-44.

'Daniël de Moulin overleden'. In: *Brabants Centrum*, 14 februari 2002.

Dessing, A.M.F., *Tulpen voor Wilhelmina. De geschiedenis van de Engelandvaarders*. Amsterdam, Uitgeverij Bert Bakker, 2004.

Faber, H. & Stolk, P., *Wij zijn niet bang, tenminste, niet erg. Het Engelandvaardersdagboek van Daniël de Moulin*. Amsterdam, DdM Works, 2015.

Faber, H., & Stolk. P., '*Het vuur smeulende houden onder de asch'. Daniël de Moulin - tussen Academie en Engelandvaart (1939-1949)*. Utrecht, Collegium Illustrissimum Hermandad, 2005.

'Gebroeders De Moulin schilderden 'Oranje Boven!' op de schoorsteen van de Gooische Stoomwasserij'. *De Bussumsche Courant*, 6 December 1962.

Heirsch-Mahler, W.H., interview by H. Faber & P. Stolk. Utrecht, 15 December 2004.

Heteren, G. van, 'In memoriam prof. dr. Daniël de Moulin (1919-2002)'. In: *Nederlands Tijdschrift voor Geneeskunde*. Volume 146 (2002), nummer 12, pp. 582-583.

Kerkhoff, A.H.M. e.a., *De Novis Inventis. Essays in the history of medicine in honour of Daniël de Moulin on the occasion of his 65th birthday*. Amsterdam-Maarssen, APA-Holland University Press, 1984.

Lieburg, M.J. van, 'In memoriam prof. dr. Daniël de Moulin. 12 September 1919 - 9 februari 2002'. In: *Nederlands tijdschrift voor heelkunde*. Aflevering 4 (2002), pp. 128-130.

Moulin-Luit, J. de, interview by H. Faber & P. Stolk. Boxtel, 4 September 2004.

Nationaal Archief: Ministerie van Justitie te Londen (Politie Buitendienst) 11904 (A.M. Berg), 12002 (J.W. Gaillard), 12132 (D. de Moulin), 12133 (P. de Moulin), 12147 (M.L. Parren), 12263 (F.J. Wilderinck) en 12695 (R.C. Kloesmeijer). Ministerie van Oorlog te Londen 2522 (P. de Moulin), 2523 (M.L. Parren), 2209 en 2535 (D. de Moulin & M.L. Parren), 2530 (R.C. Kloesmeijer), 2522, 145: 18-10-1943 nr. 27; 147: 6-11-1943 nr. 11; 156: 28-3-1944 nr. 9; 224: 1944 nr. 1055; 225: 1944 nr. 1136 (D. de Moulin). Collection losse aanwinsten betreffende de Tweede Wereldoorlog (1939-1945). Toegang 2.22.17, inventarisnummer 21.

'Oranje Boven! Huzarenstukje op Koninginnedag 1941 van de gebroeders De Moulin'. In: *De Omroeper, Historisch tijdschrift voor Naarden*. Jaargang 17 (2004), aflevering 2, pp. 64-67.

Plaquette Radboud Universiteit Nijmegen, Onderwijsgebouw Geert Grooteplein Noord 21, Nijmegen. Looproute 124.

https://philipperaichlen.wordpress.com/

Spaans-Van der Bijl, T., *Utrecht in verzet 1940-1945*. Utrecht, Stichting De Plantage, 2005.

U.S.R. Boek 1949. Utrecht, Unitas Studiosorum Rheno-Traiectina, 1949, p. 185.

Ministerie van Defensie, Bureau Registratie en Informatie Ontslagen Personeel. Uittreksel registratieve gegevens betreffende militairen, D. de Moulin, registratienr. 19.09.12.022.

Veldhuijzen, G. e.a., *Honderd jaar. De geschiedenis van de Unitasgedachte*. Utrecht, Unitas Studiosorum Rheno-Traiectina, 1979, pp. 34-35.

Walsum, Sander van, *Ook al voelt men zich gewond. De Utrechtse Universiteit tijdens de Duitse bezetting 1940-1945*. Utrecht, Universiteit Utrecht, 1995

Illustrations

Unless mentioned otherwise all illustrations are from the personal archive of Daniël de Moulin, kept in the Nationaal Archief in the Hague (his travelogue) and the Utrechts Archief in Utrecht (his photo album).

Beeldbank WO2 – NIOD: p. 31, 33, 35, 37 top, 65, 116
Utrechts Archief: p. 11
Nationaal Archief: p. 110, 114, 115, 129

Personal archives of Engelandvaarders:
Hugues Bohn (1921-2011): p. 81, 98
Robert Bourcart (1919-2011): p. 81
Jan Hubers (1924-1993): p. 60
Lodewijk Parren (1919-2006): p. 45, 78, 93, 97 right, 128, 130 top, 131, 132, 136 bottom
Philippe Raichlen (1920-1949): p. 80
Ger van der Weerd (1914-2012): p. 37 bottom

Personal archives of:
Jaques Soeterboek: p. 70, p. 134 bottom
Marc Schölvinck: p. 133

Acknowledgements

The publication and translation of De Moulin's travelogue has been made possible thanks to the help of many people. We thank them for their interest and assistance in the project and for sharing their memories about Daan, Lodewijk and Kloesje with us.

We owe a special thank you to Willemijn Oegema, the neighbour of De Moulin's widow, Janny Luit. Willemijn arranged the meeting with Mrs De Moulin-Luit and, after she had passed away, discovered the handwritten journal that she had literally saved from the bin. The vivid memories of De Moulin's friends Lodewijk Parren (†), Armand Berg (†), Hetty Heirsch-Mahler (†) and the thoughts of his widow Janny de Moulin-Luit (†) helped us to get a better idea of Daniël the person.

Maartje van de Kamp and Sierk Plantinga of the Nationaal Archief (The Hague) helped us fill in many of the blanks, and Anne Catherine Pernot identified the four Frenchmen with whom our *Engelandvaarders* crossed the Pyrenees. We would like to thank Asra, Henk and Harry, the children of Lodewijk Parren, for granting us access to the personal archive and spoken bibliography of their father.

A special thank you goes to Marc Schölvinck, son of Rolande Kloesmeijer and Felix Theodoor Schölvinck, for his interest, trust and generosity for funding this translation. Without him this book would not have been published.

The title of the original Dutch version of the book, *Wij zijn niet bang, tenminste, niet erg* was taken from a quote by Jan Willem Gaillard. Jan Willem gave the picture opposite to Daniël just before they parted ways. On the photo, it says 'we are not afraid (at least not very much so) Hendrik'. It is very likely that Hendrik described their mutual feelings and we believe that this quote reflects the content and tone of the diary.

Daniël de Moulin's travelogue journal is a literal transcription of the text that he wrote in Portugal and London. Footnotes that De Moulin later added have been incorporated into the text. One passage, which concerns the De Moulin family only and which is not relevant for the story, has been deleted.

Acknowledgements

Obvious mistakes in the chronicle have been corrected. These mainly concern names of places and people. For example, the name of the village in the region of Sens is not Clérimois but Les Clérimois and De Moulin is inconsistent in his spelling of Wim Westbroek's surname. Wilderink's official first name is Frans Johan. However, it may well be that he was called Guus among friends; that is why this has not been adapted.

The text of the second Dutch revised edition of 2015 was used for this English translation.

About the Authors

Hylke Faber (1981) studied Dutch at Utrecht University and the University of Amsterdam. He started his career as an international publisher at academic publishing house Brill and has since then been working as an (independent) publishing professional and business developer in the publishing and e-learning field.

Pieter Stolk (1978) studied pharmaceutical sciences at Utrecht University and obtained his PhD in 2008. Pieter has worked in the field of pharmaceuticals and life sciences since 2004. Besides his day job, history, in particular that of The Netherlands, Europe and United States after 1800, is a continuing passion.

Pieter and Hylke initiated and co-authored the following publications (in Dutch):

De Utrechtse student: 1945 tot nu (Utrecht Student Life: 1945 to Today). DdM Works 2018.
De Nederlandse koopvaardij in oorlogstijd (The Dutch Merchant Navy in Wartime). Boom 2014.
Klim naar de vrijheid (Climb to Freedom). www.klimnaardevrijheid.nl. Stichting DdM 2010.
Wij zijn niet bang, tenminste, niet erg (We Are Not Afraid, At Least Not Very). Stichting DdM 2006, DdM Works 2015.